What Other

Cheryl Palermo was an active member of our church, Faith Oasis Christian Center, in the 1980s in Bensalem, Pennsylvania. She was a blessing to all who knew her. As a very talented musician, Cheryl was an anointed worshipper who led many into God's presence through her music. Cheryl's love for God, His Word, and her eagerness to experience the fullness of His promises was always a living testimony to others. This book will lead the reader into a greater understanding of God's love for each of us.

Calvin & Jeannie Donald
Founding Pastors, Faith Oasis Christian Center, Bensalem, Pennsylvania

An easy read. In the story of God's redemption, Cheryl takes the reader to the back stories behind some of the most flawed individuals in the Bible to see the beauty of God's love poured out on those who struggled to live life while looking to God. You just might see yourself!

Michael Stalteri
Former Assistant Pastor, Christian and Missionary Alliance

Unusual Love Stories from the Bible is a message of hope. Life is filled with fortunate and unfortunate events. I appreciate how Cheryl Palermo communicates God's ability to bring beauty from ashes. Every page depicts God's neverending love story. This is a book worth reading.

Dr. G. Craig Lauterbach
Founder & President, Lifeword Publishing

This book will transform the way you see God and yourself. The stories within these pages reveal God's divine love, along with the grace and mercy He so generously gives to the undeserving. Thank you, Cheryl J. Palermo.

Cynthia D. Lauterbach
Vice President & CEO, Lifeword Publishing

Unusual Love Stories from The Bible is a must read. This book references strong biblical accounts and perspectives using examples of God's perfect love. In addition, this book is certainly necessary for our current culture especially for individuals who are seeking a balanced way to understand and attain fruitful relationships with a regard for true intimacy. This book will enlighten and encourage readers to pursue and persevere a path to greater understanding about unselfish love.

Navin Nandlal
Senior Pastor, New Song Worship Ministries, Pennsylvania

Cheryl Palermo has an uncanny writing ability that allows her readers to experience firsthand the message she is communicating. You will find a part of your life contained within the pages of *Unusual Love Stories from the Bible*.

Cathy Sanders
Author and Project Manager, LifeWord Publishing

Unusual
Love
Stories

FROM THE
BIBLE

God's *Unconditional* Love Revealed

C. J. Palermo

LIFEWORD
publishing

Acknowledgements

I want to thank Dr. Craig Lauterbach for believing in me as well as Pastor Gwen Mouliert who, despite a bout of COVID and the death of her beloved husband, stuck with me through the nine-and-a-half-month-long project. I would like to dedicate this book to my immediate family: Jenae, Frank, and my two grans: Jace and Jax. As readers devote themselves more fully and deeply to God they, too, will love Him more, making this world a better place for all of us.

Contents

Foreword

Another book about love, really? We know God is love, and we all can quote the famous verse John 3:16, "For God so loved the world that He gave His only begotten Son, that whoever believes in Him should not perish but have everlasting life." *So what makes this book different?* Cheryl has taken *unusual* and *unique* people in the scriptures to demonstrate the love of God.

I have been a Bible teacher for almost forty years, and working with her on this manuscript has been a pure joy! The insight that the Holy Spirit has given Cheryl has enriched my life. There were times my mouth hung open in amazement as I read the truth revealed in this book.

I fully endorse this anointed book, and I know you will be touched by the Spirit of God as these truths are revealed to you. May we all fall more and more in love with the Father, the Son, and the Holy Spirit. My prayer is that we keep the greatest commandment, Matthew 22:37-38 where Jesus said, "Thou shalt love the Lord thy God will all thy heart and with all thy soul and with all thy mind. This is the first and great commandment."

The love of God has been shed in our hearts by the Holy Spirit (Rom. 5:5), but I believe that reading this wonderful book will help each of us appreciate and appropriate how much God loves us so we can live for Him.

— Gwen Mouliert

Introduction

In 1984, the classic rock band Foreigner produced the album *Agent Provocateur* featuring the number-one hit "I Want to Know What Love Is." I was missing this aspect of my life and determined to define it. This fascination is the theme of this book. Can you honestly say you know what love is? Having been saved for 39 years, I knew love was missing from my life. I couldn't honestly say that I was an open conduit showering God's love on everyone I met. Many conversations were scripted in my mind because I knew it was God's will to plant, water, and nurture His seeds with scriptures pertaining to forgiveness, patience, etc.—but were they scripted in my heart too? First Corinthians 13 describes love beautifully, and no doubt there are countless books written on this subject. But how deep did it flow in my veins? I know "feeling" love is not the goal, even though it's nice.

Having met speaker and author Gwen Mouliert after one of her engagements, I broached this very subject. She suggested I do a word study on love using every online and available resource at my disposal. So I did just that. I wrote copious notes but it had yet to become personal for me. So I decided to study the stories and characters in the Bible. After all, they are there for a reason, right? I was amazed at what I discovered. Like a diamond, multiple facets began to shine forth, each offering a new glimmer of God's love toward us. "We love Him because He first loved us" became crystal clear as each new story unfolded. "God is love" is more than a statement. It is a fact saturated with such

11

richness and tenderness that I found myself falling headfirst in love with Him over and over again (1 John 4:10-19). Some ask, isn't this the same God who lets bad things happen? I say this is the God who steers us through bad things, prepares us, equips us, protects us, and loves us so perfectly that every detail is engineered to help us reach His ultimate goal—eternity with Him.

This is a fallen world. Satan, mankind's enemy, has spent the better part of his existence developing and encouraging the depravity of man in order to blame God for his atrocities. We must be very discerning and filled with the knowledge of God to fend off his warfare with the spiritual weapons God has given us. Gwen became my coach and dear friend leading to the completion of this book. My prayer is these pages will inspire you to read more pages leading to your own personal and intimate relationship with God Almighty, Father, Son, and Holy Ghost.

Chapter One

It's Okay to be Different: Leah and Jacob

A love story for the ages—from early childhood, every princess imagines meeting her prince at the proverbial ball where he will sweep her off her feet. Unfortunately, things didn't quite go that way for Leah. Her path was rough, and she longed for love, but no one could fulfill that need better than God Himself.

Leah's story really needs to begin with her future father-in-law, Isaac, son of Abraham, and Rebekah, Isaac's wife. It was the time in life when Isaac realized he must give his firstborn son, Esau, his blessing. So, he asked Esau to fetch game, cook up a tasty dinner, then receive his blessing. Off went Esau to the field. Rebekah, Esau's mother, overheard this conversation and quickly shared this with her other son, Jacob. Jacob, however, was not a hunter and had to rely on Rebekah's assistance to beat Esau to the blessing.

Now Esau and Jacob were fraternal twins, but Esau came out first with Jacob grasping his heel; hence the name *Jacob,* which means "he who follows after; a heeler." In hindsight, I can see courage on the part of this little one. Courage he would need later in life. Furthermore, there is another meaning to the name *Jacob*. It is *supplanter,* which means "to take the place of by treachery, deceit, or force." Jacob used deceit. He took advantage of his father's failing vision by putting animal skins on his hands and arms, as his brother was very hairy. Isaac questioned him more than once about his true identity because his voice sounded like Jacob's and the dinner arrived so quickly. However, Isaac was convinced enough to grant him the blessing. It was a very important moment that went like this:

> And may God give you of the dew of heavens and of the fatness of the earth and abundance of grain and [new] wine; Let peoples serve you, and nations bow down to you; be master over your brothers, and let your mother's sons bow down to you. Let everyone be cursed who curses you and favored with blessings who blesses you (Genesis 27:28-29).

Jacob had barely left his father when Esau arrived with a savory dinner. This came as quite a shock to both of them that Jacob would do such a thing, yet Esau remembered his brother was the supplanter, for which Esau cried, "Is he not properly named?" It would seem there is only one blessing. Notwithstanding the fact that Esau and Jacob were twins, the firstborn is the one who opens the womb. The blessing Esau received instead, by comparison, was merely kind, empty words, holding nothing of value. It also included serving his younger brother. This caused Esau to develop hatred and plot murder in his heart once their father died.

Rebekah learned of Esau's intentions and insisted Jacob flee to her brother's household over 400 miles east in Padam-Aram in Haran, today's Syria. She wanted Jacob to be safe until Esau's fury was spent, and she wanted Jacob to marry into their family. You may be wondering why Rebekah supported Jacob and not Esau. It's unclear, but Esau had already taken two foreign wives outside of the family, which made his parents' lives miserable.

Now Esau was 40 years old when he took as wife Judith the daughter of Beer the Hittite, and Basemath the daughter of Elon the Hittite. And they made life bitter and a grief of mind and spirit for Isaac and Rebekah [their parents-in-law] (Genesis 26:34-35).

Then Rebekah said to Isaac, "I'm weary of my life because of the daughters of Heth [these wives of Esau]. If Jacob takes a wife of the daughters of Heth such as these Hittite girls around here, what good will my life be to me?" (Genesis 27:46)

Along the journey, the Lord appeared to Jacob in a dream that changed him and his relationship with God forever. In his dream, God appeared to be standing above a ladder that stretched from the earth all the way to heaven. Angels were ascending and descending, which gave this the appearance of a gateway to heaven. God renewed the commitment He had made with his father (Isaac) and his father before him (Abraham) to give both him and his descendants the land on which he stood spreading in every direction. God also promised to not only bless Jacob and his seed but all the families of the earth through them, including us.

And if you are Christ's, then you are Abraham's seed, and heirs according to the promise (Galatians 3:29).

Before continuing on his journey, Jacob anointed the place where he slept by setting up a pillar and calling it *Bethel*, or "House of God."

Then he dreamed, and behold, a ladder was set up on the earth, and its top reached to heaven, and there the angels of God were ascending and descending on it. And behold, the Lord stood above it and said; …the land on which you lie I will give to you and your descendants.

Also your descendants shall be as the dust of the earth; you shall spread abroad to the west and the east, to the north and the south; and in you and in your seed all the families of the earth shall be blessed....Then Jacob awoke from his sleep and said, "Surely the Lord is in this place.... How awesome is this place! This is none other than the house of God, and this is the gate of heaven!" Then Jacob rose early in the morning and took the stone that he had put at his head, set it up as a pillar, and poured oil on top of it. And he called the name of that place Bethel (Genesis 28:12-19a).

As Jacob knew he was getting close to his destination, he chanced upon a well where three flocks were lying. He inquired of the shepherds if they knew his uncle Laban. Here is the interesting part: while they were telling Jacob that his family was well, up came Rachel, his cousin, with her father's sheep! This exact same thing happened to his father's servant, Eliezer, in search of a wife for Isaac at the same well six decades prior. This was beyond coincidence; it was exceptionally intentional.

Jumping almost one century ahead, this marriage would produce a lineage including Joseph, who saved the nation of Israel and possibly the entire known world by warning Egypt of a coming famine and protecting his family. So, no matter what the circumstances appear to be, God is in charge and has a plan. He sees the beginning from the end.

For I know the thoughts and plans that I have for you, says the Lord, thoughts and plans for welfare and peace, and not for evil, to give you hope in your final outcome (Jeremiah 29:11 AMPC).

Now, back to the story of Rachel and Jacob. Rachel was a shepherdess. Rather than make her wait until all the other shepherds had arrived, as was the practice, he rolled the huge stone off the mouth of the well and watered her sheep anyway, then kissed her! He couldn't believe his good fortune. He was so overjoyed he wept in front of all of them. It was love at first sight.

Upon arriving at Laban's, son of Bethuel, Son of Nahor, arrangements were soon made for Jacob to live and work there. He met Leah, Rachel's older sister, and the Bible tells us immediately that her eyes were weak and dull looking. Weakness implies her vision. Dull looking implies their color and shape. The additional translations lend a little more clarity. Either way, compared to Rachel, there was no comparison.

> Leah's eyes were weak and dull looking, but Rachel was beautiful and attractive (Genesis 29:17 AMPC).

> Leah had weak eyes, but Rachel had a lovely figure and was beautiful (Genesis 29:17 NIV).

> Leah was tender eyed; but Rachel was beautiful and well favoured (Genesis 29:17 KJV).

The immediate contrast with Leah's eyes and Rachel's shape and beauty is striking. Clearly, Leah did not have Rachel's looks. Leah was, no doubt, plainer in appearance than Rachel. She lacked the luster, beauty, and shapely appearance of her sister. In addition, Leah may have had a flaw—poor vision. *Rak* is the Hebrew word for "tender," which also means "weak, faint, and pitiful," which gives the impression that her vision was also weak. Important attributes such as having a heart for God, strength of character, perseverance, loyalty, diligence, trustworthiness, and transparency were not apparent at first. However, they appeared over the next 40 years. Ironically, Rachel envied Leah's ability to have children. This was demonstrated when Rachel gave Jacob her maid Bilhah to build her a family, and it shows in how she named Bilhah's children. Childbearing became an unbecoming contest between the sisters. We will revisit this shortly.

Jacob's heart was set on Rachel and he agreed to a seven-year work arrangement. Once his labor for his uncle Laban was complete, Jacob wanted to consummate his arrangement but got something quite unexpected instead. At last, the long awaited and hard-earned night had arrived. Laban arranged a little bachelor party among the boys, possibly resulting in Jacob getting a bit inebriated. Then Laban pulled the switch—Leah for Rachel. Interestingly, Leah said nothing. She went through the charade, maybe hoping against hope that Jacob wouldn't be too disappointed. Strangely, Jacob didn't realize the smooth move on Laban's part until morning. Laban's excuse for the switch was "the custom of the land." The older daughter had to be married first.

Does this sound a little, maybe a lot, like the stunt Jacob himself pulled on his father by pretending to be the older son? Laban was benefiting a lot materially. He got seven years' worth of labor out of his best employee. He was eliminating the responsibility and burden of his oldest daughter. He would negotiate another seven years of labor to his enterprise by contracting Jacob for his second daughter. He was keeping the family intact right there where he had full control of everything.

Jacob's response made it clear to Leah that he felt cheated and trampled on. No doubt he rebuked himself for not better knowing the country's customs. After all, he had seven years to learn all he could.

During all this time, he should have realized Laban was capable of anything. Laban kept changing his wages and did not keep his word. He had no loyalty to Jacob's family or his God. Still, there are other questions. Why didn't Jacob realize that was not Rachel underneath the veil? Wasn't she easier to identify, being shapelier than Leah? Was there no communication between them whereby he would recognize her voice? Where was Rachel? Was she too fearful of her dad to speak up? So, another arrangement was strong-armed. After the bridal week, Jacob would marry Rachel also but be indebted to Laban for another seven years. How must Leah have felt? This situation was forced on her, plus everyone would know her husband loved her sister more and she was neglected in her relationship.

The Lord realized Leah's predicament and had pity on her.

> And when the Lord saw that Leah was hated, he opened her womb: but Rachel was barren (Genesis 29:31).

The Hebrew word for "hated" is *sane*. It means "odious, deserving hatred, repugnant, to personally see as an enemy or foe." Wow! Why would Jacob have such hostility against her? I can only surmise that his misplaced blame fell upon her partly because she stood in the way of who he really wanted. His anger toward Laban was projected onto her. The sad part is Leah knew it too, as evidenced by the names she chose for her sons. She was the first to get pregnant. In fact, she gave birth to four sons right in a row. Bearing a son was, and still is, considered most honorable in many cultures.

> And Leah conceived, and bare a son, and she called his name Reuben: for she said, Surely the Lord hath looked upon my affliction; now therefore my husband will love me. And she conceived again, and bare a son; and said, Because the Lord hath heard that I was hated, he hath given me this son also: and she called his name Simeon. And she conceived again, and bare a son; and said, Now this time will my husband be joined unto me, because I have borne him three sons: therefore was his name called Levi, and she conceived again, and bare a son, Now will I praise the Lord; therefore she called his name Judah; and left bearing (Genesis 29:32-35).

Another way of saying "the Lord hath looked upon her affliction" is "the Lord saw her humiliation." She named him *Reuben* which means "behold a son." With the next child she said the Lord had heard that she was hated. How many times had she cried out to the Lord and felt neglected when Jacob chose to be with Rachel night after night? How awful. She named him *Simeon,* which means "hears and obeys." Because she had a third son, she truly believed Jacob would remain with her as a companion. The Hebrew word for "joined" is *lavah,* which means "to twine, to unite, to remain, abide with, cleave." She named him *Levi,* which means "adhesion." It is from the lineage of this child that the priestly kingdom was established, including musicians and caretakers of the temple and its sacred utensils for serving and sacrifice. By the time she got to the fourth there was a change. She decided to do the one thing she had not done prior to this—praise the Lord. She named this child *Judah,* which means "the Lord be praised, object of praise, praise the Lord, He shall be praised." It is from the lineage of this child that the savior of the world was presented to us some 970 years later. Innumerable books have been written on praise and worship. Let it suffice to say that there is no greater sacrifice unto the Lord than praise.

> By Him [Jesus] therefore let us offer the sacrifice of praise to God continually, that is, the fruit of our lips giving thanks to his name (Hebrews 13:15).

Leah was an interesting woman. It seemed all she wanted was for Jacob to love her and spend time with her. This is a natural feeling for most wives, but Leah included God in her choices. She even referred to Him as Lord. Her name means "wearied, tired, to be exhausted, faint from sickness." I personally think she was misnamed. Perhaps *Hayah* would have better suited her. *Hayah* means "beacon, committed, accomplished, last." You will soon see why.

It didn't help that Rachel was pushing Jacob to the limit to give her children as well.

> And when Rachel saw that she bare Jacob no children, Rachel envied her sister; and said unto Jacob, Give me

children or else I die. And Jacob's anger was kindled against
Rachel: and he said, Am I in God's stead, who hath with-
held from thee the fruit of the womb? (Genesis 30:1-2)

Rachel's motivation to have children of her own became skewed
with Leah's obvious success in that arena. She became so obsessed with
her own barrenness she insisted Jacob take Bilhah, her maid, and give
her children or build a family through her.

> And she said, Behold my maid Bilhah, go in unto her,
> and she shall bare upon my knees, that I may also have
> children by her. And she gave him Bilhah her handmaid
> to wife: and Jacob went in unto her (Genesis 30:3-4).

Bilhah conceived with her first son, Jacob's fifth, and Rachel named
him Dan because she felt vindicated. God had heard her plea. The name
Dan means "he that judges, to rule, to contend."

> And Rachel said, God hath judged me, and hath also
> heard my voice, and hath given me a son: therefore, she
> called his name Dan (Genesis 30:6).

Then Bilhah conceived again and bore Jacob a second son, Jacob's
sixth. Rachel named him Naphtali based on the belief she won the struggle between herself and her sister. The name *Naphtali* means "a struggle, my twisting, obtained by wrestling."

> And Bilhah, Rachel's maid, conceived again, and bare
> Jacob a second son. And Rachel said, with great wres-
> tlings have I wrestled with my sister and I have prevailed:
> and she called his name Naphtali (Genesis 30:7-8).

Rachel envied her sister. Envy is grieving at the good of another. At
the persuasion of Rachel, Jacob took Bilhah, her handmaid, to wife so

that, according to the usage of those times, her children might be owned as her mistress's children. Had not Rachel's heart been influenced by evil passions, she would have considered her sister's children nearer to her and more entitled to her care than Bilhah's. But she desired children whom she had a right to rule, children she could name by ownership rather than children she had more reason to love. As an early instance of her power over these children, she took pleasure in giving them names that carried in them marks of rivalry with her sister. These are the roots of bitterness, envy, and strife, which makes mischief among relations.

At the persuasion of Leah, Jacob took Zilpah, her handmaid, to wife also. Behold the power of jealousy and rivalry.[1] This contentious rivalry prompted the same immature behavior on the part of Leah. She immediately gave her maid, Zilpah, to Jacob who then bore a son, Jacob's seventh. Leah named him *Gad,* which means "good fortune." Notice, there is no mention of seeking God here. Zilpah conceived again, Jacob's eighth son, whom Leah named Asher because after a total of six sons, all the women would surely call her blessed. *Asher* means "fortunate, happy" (Gen. 30:9-13). What terrible and egotistical thinking! Evidently her bruised reputation and popularity were at stake and she wanted to redeem herself in this fashion.

God made it clear to Adam that a man shall leave his father and mother and cleave unto his wife, and they shall be one flesh (Gen. 2:24). While Leah might not have had a choice in Jacob's marriage to Rachel, surely she could have chosen not to participate in sharing her handmaiden. She did it solely for the purpose of out procreating her sister in order to earn or win Jacob's love. Yet one thing remained constant— Leah never gave up on God. She may have missed it in terms of God's will for her life, but she never abandoned Him. She instead always maintained a stubborn perseverance that God would prevail. And yet, I wonder about Jacob's ego throughout these 20 years. Was he flattered

---

1.Matthew Henry, Concise Commentary on the Whole Bible, (Chicago, Moody Press: 1983), 42-43.

beyond normal expectations or did he avoid confrontation at all costs? Did he seemingly succumb to every whim perpetrated by the sisters, especially Rachel, or did he go along to get along?

Then, of all things, the two sisters tried to hire Jacob for themselves for the price of a few mandrakes that Reuben found in the field. These herbal plants, found in the Mediterranean, bloom purple or yellow flowers. Specifically their roots, also called love apples, were said to have narcotic properties that promoted conception. Evidently, the sisters believed this myth so much so that they got into an argument as to who would get the mandrakes. Eventually, Rachel conceded to letting Jacob sleep with Leah in order to use the mandrakes herself. She basically prostituted her own husband in order to get pregnant. Where's the love? Ironically, Leah got pregnant again without the help of any plant. But Leah demanded of Jacob that he be with her because she paid for him with their firstborn's mandrakes. This is how desperate the situation had gotten between the two siblings. Also, take note of Jacob's response. He seemed to go along with everything his two wives had planned, including taking on the two secondary wives.

> And Jacob came out of the field in the evening, and Leah went out to meet him, and said, Thou must come in unto me; for surely I have hired thee with my son's mandrakes. And he lay with her that night. And God hearkened unto Leah, and she conceived, and bare Jacob the fifth son. And Leah said, God hath given me my hire, because I have given my maid unto my husband; and she called his name Issachar (Genesis 30:16-18).

> Leah became pregnant again and bore Jacob [her] sixth son. Then Leah said, God has endowed me with a good marriage gift [for my husband]; now will he dwell with me [and regard me as his wife in reality], because I have

borne him six sons; and she named him Zebulun [dwelling] (Genesis 30:19-20 AMPC).

With these new children, there were more meaningful names. *Issachar* means "wages, he brings wages, he is hired, to be rewarded." *Zebulun* means "wished for, habitation, to dwell with." How must all of these sons have felt when they put this picture together? It became pretty clear 30 years later. Sorry, that's another story for another time, or read Genesis 37 to the end—my favorite story in the whole Bible.

Finally, the last three children.

And afterwards she [Leah] bare a daughter, and she called her Dinah (Genesis 30:21).

Imagine having all those brothers. It's not certain where the only daughter of Jacob fits in between the tenth and twelfth son. Two points I would like to make here. The first point is that in the Bible, females were mainly excluded from the family lineage, with few exceptions. I believe it has to do with the "order of things" starting with the Creator God the Father, then God the Son who gives preeminence to God in all things. Then, God the Holy Spirit was given to man for a season, i.e. until the time of the Gentiles (non-Jews) is fulfilled. In order to complete His work of creation, our triune God made the ultimate masterpiece—mankind. He gave the male and female jurisdiction over every living creature (Genesis 1:26-27). Ultimately, in the shadows and examples throughout scripture, every story, including Leah's, leads to the saving grace of Jesus Christ, the Savior of the world.

And the Lord God formed man of the dust of the ground, and breathed into his nostrils the breath of life; and man became a living soul (Genesis 2:7).

And the Lord God caused a deep sleep to fall upon Adam, and he slept: and he took one of his ribs, and closed up the flesh instead thereof; And the rib, which the Lord God had taken from man, made he a woman, and brought her unto the man. And Adam said, "This is now bone of my bones, and flesh of my flesh: she shall be called Woman, because she was taken out of Man" (Genesis 2:21-23).

The second point is *Dinah,* which means "judged, vindicated, justice," was a sweet finish to Leah's childbearing years. If you were a parent of six males, wouldn't you welcome a baby girl? What a thrill to raise a precious being whom you could dress up and braid her hair every which way. Ah, why not throw in some earrings and a nose ring or two.

After the birth of Leah's daughter Dinah, Rachel's long-awaited moment had finally arrived! She conceived at nearly the age of fifty! She credited God for this long awaited miracle—the miracle of a son whom she named *Joseph,* Jacob's eleventh. The name means "may God add, He shall add, increasing." This name is a double entendre. Either this child was an addition to her legacy started by Bilhah or her eyes were already on the future. She may have been looking beyond him to the next son, which suggests a continued rivalry with her sister. Yet, he was no ordinary individual. God had huge plans for him. Joseph learned humility through many trials yet remained faithful to God and his heritage. Thirty years later, he saved the entire nation of Israel, Egypt, as well as neighboring countries. So much happened between the birth of Joseph and her only other son, Benjamin, Jacob's twelfth and last, that it took six years and five chapters to get there.

God's sovereignty was at work this entire time. At times His plans may not have always been apparent. However, it was always His intention that Jacob would sire the 12 tribes of Israel. Keep in mind that all things work together for the good of those who love God and are called according to His purpose (Romans 8:28).

Reflecting back on Rachel and Leah, both sisters were entirely motivated by jealousy. Jealousy is a sin and, when combined with bitterness, a very dangerous cocktail. When overcome with sin, everything you do, plan, and think can be shrouded in these two areas of darkness. These are some of Satan's best and oldest weapons. God knows us better than we know ourselves. It's conceivable that in their naïveté and misguided emotions, because neither sister had ever loved before, passion ruled over prudence. This could have opened a door to the real enemy. Thus, their plans, decisions, and silent competition were craftily influenced by sin. One of these women would have to pull it together in order to raise this dysfunctional family with some semblance of unity and Godly influence.

Further down the road, Rachel named her second child *Ben-oni*, which means "son of my sorrow." She knew she was dying during a difficult labor, and, unlike Joseph's birth, she focused on this baby and what he had done to her. Jacob took a stand and renamed him *Benjamin*, which means "son of the right hand, son of my days, son of my old age." Jacob, at the time, was almost 97 years old.

Overall, Rachel's story is very sad. She never learned to be content with the things God had given her—a home, beauty, Jacob's adoration, two sons, etc. She left this world in hideous pain prepared to name her second child not something rewarding and grateful but glum and depressing, reflective of a negative and unappreciated life.

Thank God Jacob changed this baby's name. Imagine yourself in Ben-oni's shoes. You would never know the intricacies of your mother's nurturing comfort and care. Additionally, every time your name was said aloud, you would be reminded of that tragic event. You would be the reminder and reason she no longer existed. Any time someone said your name, it would be as if she were constantly blaming or cursing you for her death. I suppose if Jacob were to only take one stand in his life, this was an excellent choice.

The story of Jacob is rich with details and incidents that are difficult to tell chronologically. Not only was his family growing exponentially but he played a pivotal role in the development of an entire nation. These were God's chosen people by whom He would reveal Himself to the world through the generations to come. Because this is a story about Leah, I must provide necessary imagery to convey this simple but complex lady. As time went by, Leah seemed to be growing in Jacob's esteem. History has a way of doing that. By the time they left the hill country of Gilead and had their final encounter with Laban leading to a covenant between them, Leah and Jacob had well over 20 years of history together. Now that he was past the threat of Laban, he could fully concentrate on Esau. Jacob used in-depth wisdom when he prayed to God, reminding Him of His promises. Take note of another aspect to this prayer—he included the mother with the children. Therefore, Leah had been elevated to equal status with her beautiful sister because she shared the role of being a mother to Jacob's children.

> Then Jacob said, "O God of my father Abraham and God of my father Isaac, the Lord who said to me, 'Return to your country and family, and I will deal well with you.': I am not worthy of the least of all the mercies and of all the truth which you have shown your servant; for I crossed over this Jordan with my staff, and now I have become two companies. Deliver me, I pray, from the hand of my brother, from the hand of Esau; for I fear him, lest he come and attack me and the mother with the children. For you said, 'I will surely treat you well, and make your descendants as the sand of the sea, which cannot be numbered for multitude'" (Genesis 32:9-12).

On the way back to his homeland in Canaan, after having sent his families across the brook of Jabbok, Jacob had another encounter with God. This time there was an all-night wrestling match with a "Man" who came upon him. Jacob demonstrated incredible courage and he refused to give up. (Remember we alluded to the courage he would need later on in life?) Jacob realized this was no ordinary man he was wrestling because a mere touch from Him displaced his hip. Therefore, he clung to the "Angel of the Lord" and wouldn't let Him go until he got a blessing. Jacob sure believed in collecting his rightful blessings. So the Lord gave him the blessing and desire of his heart and revealed Himself by changing his name from Jacob to Israel, from "supplanter" to "prince with God"! It doesn't get much better than that.

> Then Jacob was left alone; and a Man wrestled with him until the breaking of day. Now when He saw that He did not prevail against him, He touched the socket of his hip; and the socket of Jacob's hip was out of joint as He wrestled with him. And He said, "Let Me go, for the day breaks." But he said, "I will not let You go unless You bless me!" So He said to him, "What is your name?" He said, "Jacob." And He said, "Your name shall no longer be called Jacob, but Israel; for you have struggled with God and with men, and have prevailed" (Genesis 32:24-28).

When God touched the strongest sinew of the wrestler, it shriveled, and with it Jacob's persistent self-confidence also shriveled. His carnal weapons were lame and useless; they failed him in his contest with God. What he had surmised for the past 20 years now dawned on him: he was in the hands of the One against whom it is useless to struggle. After this crippling touch, Jacob's struggle took a new direction. Now crippled in his natural strength, he became bold in faith.[2]

At this point in time, all the children were grown, and Jacob had made peace with Esau and with Laban. There is one more event I would like to include before closing Leah's story. While on the way back to Bethel to make an altar to God, Jacob noticed that the men whose towns

---

2. John F. Walvoord and Roy B Zuck, *The Bible Knowledge Commentary*, (Colorado Springs, CO: David C Cook 1985), 81.

they passed seemed afraid of him and his caravan. God had worked in his favor and set a fear in their hearts, as He also had changed the heart of Esau and Laban. Then God appeared to Jacob and blessed him yet again. This time God reminded him of His Word. He reminded Jacob that his name was no longer Jacob, nor would he be called that anymore. He would be called Israel. The deceiver, the schemer, the supplanter no longer existed; he was now made clean. Likewise, when we become true, born-again believers we are changed into new creatures in Christ.

> Therefore, if anyone is in Christ, he is a new creation; old things have passed away; behold, all things have become new (2 Corinthians 5:17).

Like Jacob, we also will be given another name when we arrive in heaven.

> He that hath an ear, let him hear what the spirit saith unto the churches; To him that overcometh will I give to eat of the hidden manna, and will give him a white stone, and in the stone a new name written, which no man knoweth saving he that receiveth it (Revelation 2:17).

Then God told Israel His own name—God Almighty. He repeated his blessing to be fruitful and multiply, to build a nation and nations, including kings, as descendants. Then he followed up with the "promised land," which was declared the state of Israel in 1948 with its capital being recognized by the US as Jerusalem in 2020.

> And God said to him, "Your name is Jacob; your name shall not be called Jacob anymore, but Israel shall be your name." So He called his name Israel. Also God said to him: "I am God Almighty. Be fruitful and multiply; a nation and a company of nations shall proceed from you, and kings shall come from your body. This land which I

gave Abraham and Isaac I give to you; and to your descendants after you I give this land (Genesis 35:10-12).

There are times in Scripture when God changed someone's name because it did not match their character, such as in the case of Jacob. His name originally meant "heel holder" or "supplanter."[3] Jacob's name was changed to *Israel*, which means "God prevails."[4] As his name was changed, so was the way other people looked at him, and his new name was a reflection of how God helped him overcome some very difficult times. Through Jacob (Israel), God built the nation of Israel. Jacob's first wife, Leah, who was originally despised, was exalted to the extent that the tribe of Levi (the priests) and the tribe of Judah (the kings) can be traced back to her. This is a foretelling or "shadow" of things 2,050 years to come. Seem outlandish? Would it surprise you even more to see yourself in God's plan as both a king and priest? Feast your eyes on this scripture:

> And from Jesus Christ, the faithful witness, the firstborn from the dead, and the ruler over the kings of the earth. To Him who loved us and washed us from our sins in His own blood, and has made us kings and priests to His God and Father, to Him be glory and dominion forever and ever. Amen (Revelation 1:5-6).

So how does it end for Leah? Leah flourished from the inferior, weak-eyed girl, whose beautiful sister held the heart of their shared husband, to a proven mother of seven. If we consider her as the primary caregiver, counting her sister's handmaiden's sons, her handmaiden's sons, and her deceased sister's, whom Leah ironically raised as well, she raised 13 children in all! She worked through low self-esteem, jealousy,

---

3. "H3290 - ya'ăqōb - Strong's Hebrew Lexicon (kjv)." Blue Letter Bible. Accessed 5 Aug, 2022. https://www.blueletterbible.org/lexicon/h3290/kjv/wlc/0-1.
4. "H3478 - yiśrā'ēl - Strong's Hebrew Lexicon (kjv)." Blue Letter Bible. Accessed 5 Aug, 2022. https://www.blueletterbible.org/lexicon/h3478/kjv/wlc/0-1.

and superstition. She began to see God at work in her life. So did Jacob. Yes, in the first decade or two of their marriage, he only had eyes for Rachel. Yet he witnessed firsthand Leah's strength and determination to be both a good wife and mother. He saw how hard she labored and how true she remained. She was a constant in his life. It would be enough to win any man.

There is an additional point of interest I want to add, almost as a postscript. Scripture tells us that Jacob settled with his three wives, Leah being the primary wife and the two handmaidens being the secondary wives, and his 13 children in the land of Canaan. Years later, there was much animosity between Joseph and his ten older brothers. This incredible story is not part of Leah's story. However, when Joseph at the age of 17 started having dreams that wouldn't be manifested for another 13 years, Jacob, out of frustration, referenced Leah as his mother. Remember, Rachel bore Joseph, yet Leah was elevated to the status of mother for all of the children (Gen. 37:9-11).

In time, Leah softened and learned to be content with what she had. She no longer depended on Jacob to provide fulfillment. She embraced her Maker, God Almighty, who blessed her over and over. Wanting to be Jacob's favorite was abandoned for the agape love she knew and felt from God. Through perseverance and steadfastness, she earned her rightful place in the family. In time, Jacob realized Leah's inner beauty coupled with his own growth and maturity, allowing this married couple to take their rightful place in the hall of famed patriarchs.

At the end of her days, which is uncertain, but could be calculated between 75 and 85 years old, she was buried in the Cave of Machpelah near Hebron. Israel's story continued for another 17 years. This included the relocation of his family, a grand total of 70, to Egypt. After 430 years, they grew into a nation of 2,000,000 strong and returned to their beloved promised land. Jacob could have been buried in Ephrath, near Rachel; in Goshen, Egypt, where he died; in the Cave of Machpelah, where his ancestors lay; or anywhere in between. Of all the places he could have chosen, he chose to be buried in the Cave of Machpelah, *next to his wife Leah*, and next to the patriarchs—Isaac and Rebekah, Abraham and Sarah. This is a proclamation of true love—to be joined with the revered forbearers of the same promise. Truly, Leah's life is exemplified in the following:

> He gives power to the weak, and to those who have no might he increases strength. But those who wait on the Lord shall renew their strength; They shall mount up with wings like eagles, They shall run and not be weary, They shall walk and not faint (Isaiah 40:29, 31).

Chapter Two

Anyone Can Change: Rahab

The leading character in this story was constantly reminded that the God of Israel was far superior to any god she had previously worshiped. He slew kings, opened a river and a sea, and brought fear to the surrounding nations on Israel's behalf. The only clear path for her to choose was the course God laid out for her in love, which starts here with Moses.

Moses' journey was finished but not complete. He successfully led the nation of Israel out of Egypt to the brink of the promised land. Being the outstanding leader that he was, he had his successor lined up and ready to go. The next leader would be Joshua. He was such a good student with years of loyalty and prowess that the first personage to be named in the Bible is him. One can understand this because he led over two million people into unknown territories, all ruled by different kings, to fight for their promised inheritance. Following in the footsteps of Moses would be difficult enough, but to assume leadership over a nation almost equivalent to the population of Houston, Texas would take nerves of steel. It could not be done without God and Joshua knew it.

Originally, he was named Hoshea or Oshea, son of Nun, eighth generation from Ephraim, son of Joseph, son of Jacob, son of Isaac, son of

Abraham. Moses renamed Oshea when he originally sent the 12 spies, all being leaders of their tribes, into the land of Canaan.

> These are the names of the men whom Moses sent to spy out the land. And Moses called Hoshea the son of Nun, Joshua (Numbers 13:16).

Oshea was now Joshua. The Hebrew derivative is *Jeshua* or *Jesus*. *Jesus* means "salvation, Jehovah saved." The Greek form of *Joshua* is *Jesus*. It means "Yahweh saves" or "Yahweh is salvation" He was a type of Jesus the Christ.[5] We will see why later in the story.

Let's quickly review Joshua's story. At the age of 84, he gathered the second generation of Israel and established their loyalty by reminding them of all the things God had done and would continue to do under his leadership. This monumental period of less than 20 years would involve all 12 tribes conquering their land, whose borders and boundaries were outlined in detail by God Himself. God, in turn, would usher them to victory over and over again. Canaan would become Israel, the promised land.

> Saying, "To you I will give the land Canaan, as the allotment of your inheritance," When you were few in number, indeed very few, and strangers in it. When they went from one nation to another, And from one kingdom to another people, He permitted no man to do them wrong; Yes He rebuked kings for their sakes (1 Chronicles 16:18-21).

They started at Jericho. The small "City of Palms" was smack dab in the path of the central highlands of the Jordan Valley in the Judean Desert. It was halfway between the north tip of the Sea of Chinneroth (Sea

---

5. William Smith, *Smith's Bible Dictionary, Complete Concordance* (Nashville, TN: Holman Bible Publication, 1960), 168.

of Galilee) and the south base of the Salt Sea (Dead Sea). The Israelites were camped in Shittim, otherwise known as the Acacia Grove, due east of the Jordan River and just north of Mt. Nebo where Moses had recently died. Upon crossing the river, they had to go through Jericho to go anywhere else.

Joshua thought it wise to size up the city by inspecting the weak parts of the walls and gates and to observe what the city's forces and plans were. So, he sent messengers, just as he had been sent by Moses 40 years prior, but there was one major difference. Instead of one from each tribe, he sent only two messengers avoiding the risk of a diverse report. He sent brave men willing to risk their lives for this critical information. Very strategic.

It's here in Jericho that we meet Rahab. She was a Canaanite living on the front wall. Often, two barrier walls twelve to fifteen feet apart insulated the outside wall. People put boards across and built a type of dwelling for themselves. Rahab was fortunate—she had a window. This was no coincidence, as we will soon see. She made her living right there in her own house as a harlot. The institution of prostitution goes back to the beginning of time.

Joshua's messengers didn't just happen upon Rahab's lodging. Many reasons are proffered:

1. Being a well-known harlot, men were coming and going regularly.

2. After the scouts strolled nonchalantly around the enclosed city, they casually worked their way to Rahab's place.

3. Her place was on the wall for a quick getaway.

4. Divine providence.

I think you already know the answer. God guides and directs our steps in great detail, yet not against our will.

In all thy ways acknowledge Him, and He shall direct
thy paths (Proverbs 3:6).

Let's take a hard look at *Rahab* for a second. Her name means
"proud, broaden, at liberty, a woman of Jericho, a Canaanitess." As
a proud woman of Jericho she wanted to widen her and her family's
chance of survival. She quickly and courageously took command of an
unexpected situation in which she was also quick to think on her feet.
Amazingly, she exhibited no fear of the scouts. If she was afraid, she
didn't show it. She did, however, acknowledge that she and her fellow
tribesmen were scared to death and had already mentally succumbed
to defeat.

> Now before they lay down, she came up to them on the
> roof, and she said to the men, I know that the Lord has
> given you the land, and that your terror is fallen upon us,
> and that all the inhabitants of the land faint because of
> you. For we have heard how the Lord dried up the water
> of the Red Sea for you, when you came out of Egypt, and
> what you did to the two kings of the Amorites who were
> on the [east] side of the Jordan, Sihon and Og, whom you
> utterly destroyed. When we heard it, our hearts melted,
> neither did spirit or courage remain any more in any
> man, because of you; for the Lord your God, He is God
> in heaven above, and on earth beneath (Joshua 2:8-11).

She had the composure and quick wittedness to negotiate with them
for her safety and the safety of her family. She did this before laying
out a logical course of action for them to escape undetected; hide in
the mountains, which were in the opposite direction; then backtrack to
their own camp three days later. Meanwhile, the king sent soldiers to
capture the Hebrew spies after having learned of their alleged arrival to
her "inn." Rahab intentionally misdirected them toward the river. Curi-
ously, they were not suspicious enough to either search her house or

interrogate her. This proved costly to the Canaanites. She then wasted no time getting the Israelite scouts down from their hiding place under flax stalks drying on the roof. All this time, her life was in grave danger by trusting and harboring enemies of her people, aiding and abetting their escape, and bringing her whole family to one place while they awaited the desired outcome. Why did she choose the Israelites over her own people? I think the answer has already been revealed. She believed Israel's God could and would conquer Jericho's gods.

> Now therefore, I beg you, swear to me by the Lord, since I have shown you kindness, that you also will show kindness to my father's house, and give me a true token, and spare my father, my mother, my brothers, my sisters, and all that they have, and deliver our lives from death." So the men answered her, "Our lives for yours, if none of you tell this business of ours. And it shall be, when the Lord has given us the land, that we will deal kindly and truly with you." (Joshua 2:12-14).

As promised, the Israelite scouts reported everything they had learned, which was quite different from the original report. This information was so important that it traveled from Joshua to the high priest, Eleazar, to all of the leaders. There was still much to do before the taking of Jericho, not the least of which included the miraculous crossing of the Jordan. The Lord cut off the water so that it stood in a heap. He performed a similar miracle for their parents at the Red Sea.

> When the people left their tents to cross the Jordan, headed by the priests who carried the ark of the compact (covenant), as soon as the bearers reached the Jordan and the feet of the priests dipped in the water at the edge (for the Jordan overflows all its banks during the whole time of harvest) the waters that flow down stopped and were dammed up at a distance, at Adamah, while the waters

that flow away to the sea of the Arabah (the salt sea) were cut off and failed. In this way the people crossed, opposite Jericho. The priests who carried the ark of the compact of the Eternal stood still on dry ground until the whole nation finished crossing (Joshua 3:14-17).

We have a time stamp of the tenth day of the first month (Aviv, March/April) when the people set up their new camp in Gilgal east of the Jordan and a few miles south of Jerusalem in the Jericho plain. Joshua took this time to consecrate his people through the covenanted act of circumcision. Adults typically take two to three weeks to recover from this procedure.

Meanwhile, a great fear of the Israeli people was spreading all throughout the country and coastal region.

So it was, when all the kings of the Amorites who were on the west side of the Jordan, and all the kings of the Canaanites who were by the sea, heard that the Lord had dried up the waters of the Jordan from before the children of Israel until we had crossed over, that their heart melted; and there was no spirit in them any longer because of the children of Israel. (Joshua 5:1)

Another time stamp was observed—the 14th day of Aviv, the month of Passover. The Hebrew people tasted the produce of the land for the first time. How sweet it must have been, knowing they were eating from the land of milk and honey, which was about to become their own. As if to prove they were now home, heaven no longer rained down the manna they had eaten for forty years.

Then the ultimate miracle of all, Christ incarnate visited Joshua.

And it came to pass, when Joshua was by Jericho, that he lifted his eyes and looked, and behold, a Man stood opposite him with His sword drawn in His hand. And Joshua went to Him and said to Him, "Are you for us or for our adversaries?" So He said, "No, but as Commander of the army of the Lord I have now come." And Joshua fell on his face to the earth and worshiped, and said to Him, "What does my Lord say to His servant?" Then the Commander of the Lord's army said to Joshua, Take your sandal off your foot, for the place where you stand is holy," And Joshua did so (Joshua 5:13-15).

Scripture doesn't tell us, but it is clear Joshua already knew the plan. He spoke with God regularly. Jesus coming there as Commander provided the support and confidence Joshua and his people needed to begin this long, arduous journey. God told Joshua that Jericho was already delivered into his hands—the enemy was already defeated! What confidence Joshua must have had as he went into battle! Christians also fight against a defeated enemy. Our enemy, Satan, has been defeated by Christ at the cross.[6]

Now the critical time to take Jericho down had finally arrived. Each day, for six consecutive days, 40,000 men of war led the procession. Behind them were seven priests blowing shofars or trumpets of rams' horns, followed by the ark of the Lord and its rearguard. The seventh day, however, was different. At the crack of dawn, they repeated their former manner of encircling the city but did it seven times consecutively, as if to say the ceremonial aspect of their demise was completed. Under Joshua's strict orders, no one would shout or let their voice be heard until he instructed them to do so.

But before the shouts began, Joshua's previous spies in Jericho were sent to gather Rahab and her family. Earlier reference was made to the window Rahab was fortunate to have. The spies were able to identify the window of her dwelling by a red cord that hung there. This prevented

---

6. Footnote for Joshua 6:2-5, *New King James Version: Life Application Study Bible* (United States: Tyndale House Publishers, Incorporated, 1996), 344.

the mistake of the scouts going to the wrong residence. She and her family were saved, just as the spies had promised. Time was of the essence. She lived on the wall and that wall was coming down fast! Did you ever notice that God's timing is perfect?

Finally came a new command:

> Shout for the Lord has given you the city! Now the city shall be doomed by the Lord to destruction, it and all who are in it. Only Rahab the harlot shall live, she and all who are with her in the house, because she hid the messengers that we sent (Joshua 6:16b-17).

After further instructions to only take the consecrated things for the treasury of the Lord such as gold, silver, bronze, and iron, the Israelites were ready to stampede. The priests blew the animal horns, and in the heat of excited anticipation they all shouted, and the wall fell down flat!

Can you imagine the invisible angels standing in place ready to push the walls upon command? Now this was no ordinary wall. In some places, Jericho had fortified walls up to 25 feet high and 20 feet thick. Soldiers standing guard on top of the walls could see for miles. Jericho was a symbol of military power and strength—the Canaanites considered it invincible.[7] Once the successful battle was over, Rahab and her people were taken to a place "outside of the camp" where life for her would dramatically change.

Rahab's story is directly tied to Joshua's story. We are about to leave Joshua as we project into the future. He has been called a type of Jesus. How, you may ask? Let's look at Jesus first then ask if Joshua simulated any of these attributes. Jesus came to be the true expression of the Father. He was solely motivated by chaste and pure intentions.

---

7. Footnote for Joshua 6:1, *New King James Version: Life Application Study Bible* (United States: Tyndale House Publishers, Incorporated, 1996), pg. 344.

> Who being the brightness of His glory, and the express image of His person, and upholding all things by the word of His power, when he had by Himself purged our sins, sat down on the right hand of the Majesty on high (Hebrews 1:3).

Joshua only cared about following in the footsteps of his predecessor, Moses. After having served and shadowed Moses for all of his adult life, he learned patience by obediently "going around that mountain again" for 40 more years. He served flawlessly and spent every day of his life helping God's people. He learned responsibility and developed his God-given leadership qualities. He had the highest integrity and was honest and faithful. He communed with God regularly.

Jesus never deviated from this path even when He knew going to Jerusalem would mean His undoing.

> Jesus saith unto them, My meat is to do the will of Him
> that sent me, and to finish His work (John 4:34).

Joshua maintained the conviction that his role was to bring God's people into the promised land, in which he succeeded admirably. No enemy would intimidate or delay God's purpose for his life. He was a straight arrow—dedicated, committed, and virtuous. He believed God. He undertook the almost impossible task of leading a nation for at least 20 years in the latter part of his life.

Jesus came to save the lost.

> For the son of man is come to save that which is lost (Matthew 18:11).

Joshua purposed to bring every last person into their own homeland with integrity and true grit. Joshua not only led his people literally into the promised land, but he led them spiritually as well. His final farewell to all of the tribes of Israel went like this:

> Now therefore, fear the Lord, serve Him in sincerity and in truth, and put away the gods which your fathers served on the other side of the river and in Egypt. Serve the Lord! And if it seems evil to you to serve the Lord, choose for yourselves this day whom you will serve, whether the gods which your fathers served that were on the other side of the river, or the gods of the Amorites, in whose land you dwell. But as for me and my house, we will serve the Lord (Joshua 24:14-15).

As Joshua led Israel to victory over her enemies and into possession of the promised land, and as he interceded for the nation after it had sinned and been defeated, so does Jesus. He brings the people of God into a promised rest.[8]

Little did Joshua know that his Lord and Savior would share the same name.

Now back to Rahab. Rahab was well known as a harlot or prostitute. This fact is recorded six times in the Bible, including the New Testament. How does one overcome the stigma and the guilt that goes with it? It's not easy, but God mercifully covers a multitude of sins (1 Pet. 4:8).

Once your life goes in another direction after true repentance, people forget the former you or the "old man." They don't see you as the former you but the new you.

> Therefore, if anyone is in Christ, he is a new creation; old things have passed away; behold, all things have become new (2 Corinthians 5:17).

---

8. John F. Walvoord and Roy B Zuck, *The Bible Knowledge Commentary*, (Colorado Springs, CO: David C Cook 1985), 326.

Stop right here. When reading the writings of the apostle Paul, do you see him as Paul or Saul from Tarsus who persecuted the Christians? Get to that place where you only care about what God thinks. This requires maturation through dedication to Him and His Word. Let God be your country and the Bible be your flag.

Let's analyze why Rahab was kept "outside the camp." Being placed outside the camp was for a specific reason. For example, Moses pitched the tabernacle of meeting outside the camp. This contained the sanctuary in one part and the ark in another. Here God revealed Himself to Moses.

> Moses took his tent and pitched it outside the camp, far from the camp, and called it the tabernacle of meeting. And it came to pass that everyone who sought the Lord went out to the tabernacle of meeting which was outside the camp (Exodus 33:7).

There is also an even deeper significance to being "outside the camp." It pertains to blood. Sin offerings (sins against man and oneself) and trespass offerings (sins against God) such as the sacrifice of bulls, rams, goats, lambs, turtle doves, and pigeons temporarily atoned for man's sins. These sacrifices provided a symbolic atonement and restoration to God. The only sin offering, however, that could provide true cleansing from sin and forgiveness was the death and crucifixion of Jesus Christ, the Son of God (Heb. 9:9-15).

So, what does all this talk about sacrifices have to do with Rahab? Clearly, she had a lot of adjusting to do. She would need to find strength in her character to withstand the stigma and reputation she had brought on herself and her family. She was in the right place to do it. She was outside the camp. Here she was respected as the woman who bravely saved their nation. How did she change from a tough, independent woman with no loyalty to any particular god to a righteous woman who married an Israelite prince in the short term and whose faith was compared to Abraham's in the long term?

There is nothing recorded to indicate Rahab's distaste for her former lifestyle other than the fact that from the time she was rescued her life habits and livelihood changed. Many people are content with their sinful habits and vices because they believe God is a good God and will look the other way. They might also fool themselves by comparing their ways to "bigger" sinners such as murderers, rapists, felony larcenists, and the like. After all, they don't hurt anybody. They even do good for others and attend church. All sin, big or small, has one thing in common—it separates us from God.

> But your iniquities have separated you from your God;
> And your sins have hidden His face from you, so that He
> will not hear (Isaiah 59:2).

Comparing ourselves to others is obsolete. *"For all have sinned, and fallen short of the glory of God"* (Rom. 3:23). We are only deceiving ourselves. All of us have sinned except one person. How can we know who the one person is who never sinned?

> For the wages of sin is death, but the gift of God is eternal life in Christ Jesus our Lord. (Romans 6:23)

This gift is just that—a gift—and like any present you can accept it or reject it. What makes this gift so special? This gift is a life—God's life in exchange for yours. He laid down His short life here on the earth for all who want to live eternally with Him and everything wonderful that is in heaven (Matt. 20:28b). This was Jesus' main purpose for coming into the world as we have already seen. Good works cannot save you or justify your sins.

This is going to take faith on your part. I know it sounds risky. Abraham took the leap. He chose to believe God and he became the father of both the Jews and the Arabs, and of all those who believe (Rom. 4:3-5, 10, 13 and Gal. 3:26, 29). The Bible says faith is the reality, manifestation, invisible material, assurance, confidence, conviction of what we have asked for yet have not seen. It's believing—better yet, knowing—you'll receive what you have prayed for. It's the first step in the transfer of the spiritual to the natural world. It's an agreement between you and God that aligns both His word and His will (Heb. 11:1).

But faith alone is not enough. There needs to be action. The biblical example is as follows:

> What does it profit, my brethren, if someone says he has faith but does not have works? Can faith save him? If a brother or sister is naked and destitute of daily food, and one of you says to them, "Depart in peace, be warmed and filled," but you do not give them the things which are needed for the body, what does it profit? Thus, also faith by itself, if it does not have works, is dead (James 2:14-17).

The example used a little further in the chapter is when father Abraham, by faith, offered up Isaac his son at God's bidding, believing God would raise him from the dead. Because he knew even at 100 years old he would someday become the father of many nations with a surprise bonus of becoming the first to be called God's friend (James 2:21-24). Just as the body without a spirit (breath) is dead, so is faith without deeds (James 2:26).

Of all the faithful characters in both the Old and New Testament—including the patriarchs, the immediate family of Jesus, the disciples, most of whom were persecuted to the death because of their faith, the apostle Paul who wrote two thirds of the New Testament, and early believers who spread Christianity all over the world—God chose Rahab. The scripture says it best:

> Likewise, also was not Rahab, the harlot, justified by works, when she had received the messengers, and had sent them out another way? (James 2:25)

Rahab the harlot proved by her works that she was justified by true faith like Abraham, therefore also worthy to be called God's friend. Despite her previous sinful life, her faith is compared to Abraham's! Instead of *likewise* other translations use "In like manner" or "in the same manner." One of only two women, she too made it into the Hall of Faith otherwise known as the Hall of Heroes. She is at home with other biblical heroes such as Isaac, Jacob, and Moses, not to mention David, Samuel, the prophets, and women who received their dead by resurrection and many others "of whom the world was not worthy." She is listed in the Hall of Faith immediately after the kind of faith it took for the Israelite army to shout the huge wall of Jericho down.

What could be better than all of this acknowledgement? Just one thing more—she was an important link in the lineage of the greatest Man to ever step foot on the face of the earth. It was practically unimaginable for a woman of her lowly ranking to think she might be chosen to be in the royal lineup of the one most desired, the Savior of the world, the Messiah, the King of kings, God the Son.

We asked earlier, what made Rahab change? While outside the camp, she witnessed and lived a sanctified life, making her former way of life nothing more than a blurred memory. Rather than be used and then rejected, she was respected as the woman who stood up against great odds to save God's people. They knew if Joshua thought enough of her to include her in the final set of instructions before their first conquest of taking down Jericho's walls, she must be special.

However, at what point did she make Israel's God her God? God works through people—like Rahab—whom we are inclined to reject. God remembered her because of her faith, not her profession. Rahab rose above her situation through her trust in God.[9] She heard, witnessed, and experienced many miracles, all related to Israel's God. Her heart began to soften. Her fear turned to reverence. Then she met Salmon, a Judean prince, and married him. Rahab became the wife of Salmon, a prince of Judah, and so a mother in the royal line of David and Jesus.[10] As per the genealogy of Jesus Christ written in Matthew, there are three women named and one referenced.

> The book of the genealogy of Jesus Christ, the son of David, the son of Abraham...Judah begot Perez and Zerah by Tamar...Salmon begot Boaz by Rahab, Boaz begot Obed by Ruth (Matthew 1:1-2,5).

Rahab was listed number two and her daughter-in-law, Ruth, was number three. Salmon was sixth in line from his ancestor Judah and fourth in line as an ancestor to David, the greatest king of Israel. It is through David's lineage we can trace the ancestry of Jesus. Through David's son Nathan, the lineage goes to Mary's father, Heli, and then through David's other son, Solomon, the lineage goes to Joseph's father, Jacob.

We find out later on in Matthew 1:17 that there were 14 generations from Abraham to David, 14 generations from Solomon to Josiah, and 14 generations from the deportation to Babylon to Jacob, Joseph's father. Joseph was the legal and earthly father of Jesus and husband of Mary, mother of Jesus. Sounds like God had a plan.

Rahab's legacy is a shining testimony to God's mercy and faithfulness that knows no bounds. He is faithful even when we are faithless.

---

9. Insert about Rahab, *New King James Version: Life Application Study Bible* (United States: Tyndale House Publishers, Incorporated, 1996), 341.

10. William Smith, *Smith's Bible Dictionary, Complete Concordance* (Nashville, TN: Holman Bible Publication, 1960), 257.

If we are faithless, He remains faithful; for He cannot deny Himself (2 Timothy 2:13).

He loves us all the same. Ultimately, this is a love story between Rahab and Israel's God who became her God, your God, and mine.

Chapter Three

I Believe in You: Samson and His Parents

P arents who are too loving can be the most stubborn set of people in the world. They do not give up. Their love transcends life itself. They just never quit. Such was the case of the parents of one of Israel's great judges. They saw in their son a redeemer. They died with that vision stored deep in their hearts.

Samson was conceived in a lowly time for Israel (710 B.C.). There had been so much debauchery and idolatry that God released them into the hands of their arch enemy, the Philistines, for the next 40 years. During the quest to conquer the promised land, the Philistines of the southern region, specifically the tribe of Dan's allotment, were ruthless and considered the toughest to conquer. They thought nothing of gouging your eyes out or even burning you alive, as we will unfortunately soon see. However, let's not get ahead of ourselves.

The Philistines lived on the west side of Canaan, along the Mediterranean seacoast. From Samson's day until the time of David they were the major enemy in the land and a constant threat to Israel. The Philistines were fierce warriors; they had the advantage over Israel in numbers, tactical expertise, and technology. They knew the secret of making weapons out of iron.[11]

During this time, Samson was born to a dignified couple, Manoah, well respected among his peers, and Mrs. M, his wife, a woman of integrity. One day an angel, no ordinary angel, appeared to Mrs. M. His appearance was like that of "an Angel of God, very awesome" (Judg. 13:6a).

His message was even more startling. The Man of God announced to Mrs. M, who was barren, that not only would she conceive but she must restrict alcohol and "unclean food" from her diet, as that of a Nazirite because her son would be "a Nazirite to God from the womb to the day of his death" (Judg. 13:7).

This was unusual because the angel not only appeared twice to Mrs. M but epiphanies of this nature, i.e. face to face, had only happened to one other woman. Hagar, the Egyptian maidservant to Sarah, Abraham's wife, ran from her presence into the wilderness. The Angel of the Lord spoke directly to her and gave her a wonderful promise of posterity for her son Ishmael: "'Return to your mistress, and submit yourself under her hand.' Then the Angel of the Lord said to her, 'I will multiply your descendants exceedingly, so that they shall not be counted for multitude'" (Gen. 16:9-10). At another time, an angel spoke from heaven to encourage and refresh her.

On the other hand, one could argue that the Angel of the Lord appeared to Sarah *but* the incarnation of Christ was there to meet with her husband Abraham. When he did appear, she laughed at the incredulous promise she overheard given to Abraham of giving them a son in their old age—her 90 and him 100. The Angel rebuked her while standing inside the tent. Yikes. I would hate for that to happen to me, wouldn't you? That was a bittersweet day for Sarah. Another appearance

---

11. Footnote for Judges 13:1, *New King James Version: Life Application Study Bible* (United States: Tyndale House Publishers, Incorporated, 1996), 410.

to a future mother or even a woman did not occur again until Gabriel appeared to Mary, the future mother of Jesus.

All of Judges 13 is dedicated to the conversation between Manoah and Mrs. M. Communication and trust is key in a good relationship. When Manoah's prayer was answered and the Angel of the Lord returned a second time, Mrs. M ran to get Manoah. He quickly discovered that she had relayed the encounter accurately. If there was any doubt on his part regarding her story it changed when the Angel affirmed he was the same Man who spoke to her before. The Angel then repeated His commands to her. Manoah's job was to "let her do it"—in other words, support her. Therefore, their first act of love was to serve as a Nazirite household to their as yet unborn son.

I thought about why the Angel may have gone directly to Mrs. M. Becoming a Nazirite in order to give birth to a Nazirite was a command, but it was also her choice as it is for all Nazirites. In this sense, I agree she had a choice over her own body but not the life of another inside her. The sanctification process was very specific. Mrs. M was "to be careful" not to drink wine or alcohol, eat anything from the vine, or eat anything unclean. In addition, the child was forbidden to shave any hair from his head. The Angel also revealed the gender and purpose for this special child; he would "begin" to deliver Israel from the Philistines (Judg. 13: 3-5).

Let's return to the life of a Nazirite for a long moment. The restrictions always included abstaining from alcohol, avoiding unclean food, not shaving one's head, and not becoming ritually impure by contact with corpses or graves. Interestingly enough, there are very few Nazirites in the Bible. Specifically there are:

Two examples of Nazirites in the Hebrew Bible are Samson (Judges 13:5) and Samuel (1 Samuel 1:11). Both were born of previously barren mothers and entered into their vows through either their mothers' oath (as in the case of Hannah) or a divine command (in the case of Samson) rather than by their own volition. These vows required Samson and Samuel to live devout lives, yet in return they received extraordinary gifts: Samson possessed strength and ability in physical battle against the Philistines, while Samuel became a prophet.

Some believe that Samson broke his vow by touching the dead body of a lion and drinking wine (Judg. 14:8-10). However, the divine terms for not touching a dead body, listed in Numbers 6, refer to the body of a human—not that of an animal. Also, the feast held by Samson for his marriage does not indicate that Samson drank wine. In addition, the supernatural strength that Samson was given would have been taken away at the time of Judges 14 if his Nazirite vow had been broken.[12]

Removing the tunics from the dead bodies of the thirty Philistines he killed in Ashkelon would have broken the Numbers 6 law. "Samson has a unique Nazirite status called Nazir Shimshon which permitted him to touch dead bodies, since the angel who imposed the status omitted this restriction."[13]

A closer look at the laws of Numbers 6 and the story of Samson in Judges 13–16 reveals far more differences than similarities. Samson's hair is the key to his role as deliverer of his people from the Philistines— the task for which he was consecrated. When his hair was cut, he was no longer able to deliver even himself from the enemy. It was only once his hair had begun to grow back that he might ask for strength to bring the temple down (Judg. 16:28-30). This is similar to the response to inadvertently coming into contact with a corpse, after which the person must shave the head twice before reconsecrating it by ceasing to shave (Num. 6:9-12). While both texts prohibit the consumption of alcohol, the prohibition in Judges is only incumbent upon Samson's mother (Judg. 13:4, 7, 14), not on the Nazirite himself, as is the case in Numbers 6:3-4.

---

12. "Nazirite," *Wikipedia*, last modified June 18, 2022, https://en.wikipedia.org/wiki/Nazirite.
13. Ibid.

Perhaps more significant to the story of Samson is that he killed many Philistines. He killed 30 Ashkelonians (Judg. 14:19), some in revenge for the deaths of his wife-to-be and her father (Judg. 15:8), and a thousand with the jawbone of an ass (Judg. 15:15-16). This put him in the presence of dead bodies, expressly in contradiction to the laws in Numbers 6:6-7. The Samson story describes a liminal hero, sitting on the edge of what is acceptable and what is not. His behavior is troubling not only to modern readers but also to his own compatriots (Judg. 14:3; 15:10-13). He was far from the ideal leader. He was violent and short-tempered; he was rather promiscuous, and he wished to marry outside his kin group. More than this, however, his consecration as a Nazirite seemed to weigh on him so heavily that he willingly revealed his secret to the enemy.[14]

Samson, one of the few named Nazirites in the Bible, was set apart from his own people, but his unique, life-long vow as a Nazirite was to deliver his people from their most notorious enemy, the Philistines. So, when the subject came up regarding not touching dead bodies, I ask how could he have done both? We know he killed the lion in self-defense—kill or be killed (Judg. 14:5-6a). The Spirit of the Lord came upon him for that purpose. He also killed thousands of Philistines, which placed him as a hero in the New Testament. God never puts us in compromising positions. He equips us to win and succeed in order to glorify Him.

Sanctification is a similar type of dedication to a holy lifestyle. To consecrate one's life is to omit everything that hinders or prevents someone from walking closely with the Lord. To consecrate one's life is to set yourself apart from every distraction in life that could hold you back or, worse, separate you from God's purpose for your life. Samson's purpose was to *begin* to deliver Israel single-handedly from the Philistines. Samuel's part, as a prophet and a judge, was to defeat and hold the Philistines back by sanctifying his people.

---

14. "Samson: What Kind of Nazirite Was He?," Ely Levine, TheTorah.com, accessed July 7, 2022, https://www.thetorah.com/article/samson-what-kind-of-nazirite-was-he.

* * *

Samuel Subdues the Enemy

The Nazirite prophet Samuel played a huge part in defeating the Philistines after Samson's death. Samuel cleaned up the existing idolatry by having the house of Israel put away their foreign gods and goddesses and return to the Lord with all their hearts. They confessed their sins and agreed to serve Him only. Samuel gathered them together and prayed for them. The Philistines heard of their gatherings, but Samuel also offered a holocaust—a whole burnt offering of a lamb. When the Philistines drew near to battle, the Lord answered Samuel with deafening thunder, creating such vast confusion that the Israelites overcame them and drove them back (1 Sam. 7:3-11).

* * *

Finally, Samson was born. Mrs. M named him *Samson,* which means "strong, sunshine, sunlight, distinguished, a perfect servant." This is just as good a place as any to insert Samson's improprieties, because everyone knows he was not the perfect servant. Did his mother misname him? We'll see.

For the 50 or fewer years he lived, he only traveled a total of 35 square miles. He loved two women, one of whom was his wife, with whom the marriage itself may not have even been consummated. It barely lasted a week. The second woman was a hardcore prostitute who would do anything if the price was right. He executed probably 6,500 or more Philistines without sword or arrow in his lifetime. He was born into a Nazirite role. His only instructors were his loving and adoring parents and his heritage. He was a strapping young fellow with a godly mission on his shoulders. To live up to his name as a "perfect servant," he would have needed therapeutic training to overcome his weaknesses, which were anger and women. Yet God works all things together for the good of those who fulfill His purpose (Rom. 8:28).

God used Samson's anger for His purpose and Samson's lust for His discipline. I have found in my 39-year walk with Christ that the best way to avoid committing the same sins over and over is to avoid the forbidden fruit. This could be a literal place, a physical tendency, or an image within your mind. A smutty scene on TV, a magazine, picture, etc. can trigger thoughts that will return over and over. Turn your eyes away. Redirect your thoughts to something else. Don't give place to condemnation or you won't be able to continue the Lord's work. Begin praising the Lord. Stay pure in your thoughts and life or else temptation will return when you're most vulnerable.

While he may not have directly broken his Nazirite vows, through sin (moral infirmities) he opened the door of opportunity Satan needed to "cash in." Obviously, sins and vows are two different things. We are not to make vows lightly. It is important to let our yays be yays and our nays be nays at all costs (Matt. 5:33-37).

Samson grew up a bit willful, almost insolent. He liked doing things his way, often outside of his loving parents' advice. As a late teenager he ventured into Philistine territory and saw someone who was easy on the eyes. He found her in Timnah about six miles southeast of Zorah, his hometown. As an impressionable young man, he just had to have her—as his wife no less. His parents tried to dissuade him by suggesting he choose from among his own kind. His short fuse of a temper wasn't having any of it. He insisted Dad take him back and make arrangements with her family. Reluctantly, both parents accompanied him because either way he was going back to marry her. Can any parents out there relate to older children who selectively listen and consider your loving advice even less? If only we were more like God in these instances, myself included. But God was already prepared to use Samson's willfulness (Judg. 14:1-4).

Something interesting happened next. Along the way, a young lion jumped out of nowhere and tried to attack Samson. This may have been the first time Samson realized just how strong he really was. God was prepared. He is omniscient. The Spirit of the Lord came upon him and gave him superhuman strength to tear apart a young lion limb from limb bare-handed. I estimate a young male venturing away from its pride to be on average over six feet long and roughly 450 to 500 pounds.

So, arrangements were made between the families for a wedding feast. Thirty Philistine male "companions" were invited by her family as sort of an added protection in case there was any trouble (Judg. 14: 10-11).

This event precipitated a rather clever riddle Samson devised. It was about honey he found in the carcass of the lion he killed previously. Three days into the wedding celebration, the "companions" were no closer to unlocking the riddle. So they did what they did best and threatened to kill the young bride and her family if she didn't get the secret from Samson. She began begging him to tell her the answer. His initial response was, "Look, I didn't even tell my parents; am I going to tell you?" Evidently, parents were given first place in the family. Women were in many ways subservient to men. She, however, wore him down after seven days of constant weeping. This wedding started to become anything but joyful. She shared the answer with the Philistines who, in turn, shared it with Samson. When he found out, his anger at all of them was so rampant that he immediately left, went to Ashkelon, and killed 30 total strangers for the garments he now owed the wedding companions. Notice as mad as he was, he still honored the bet. Then he went home to his parents (Judg. 14:19-20).

No doubt his parents took him in and consoled him. But they couldn't keep him there for long. He had a taste of blood, so to speak, and around the time of the wheat harvest Samson wanted to be with his wife. When he arrived at his father-in-law's house to reunite with her, he was told that she was given to his "best friend" because the father thought Samson hated her. Then, like a slap in the face, he offered Samson his younger daughter instead. Anyone in this situation would be furious, let alone someone like Samson, considering the magnitude of his strength and bad temper. He was like dynamite with a very short fuse.

Again, his retaliation was directed toward the Philistines in general, not just his father-in-law. He tied 300 foxes together by their tails, stuck fire torches between the tails, lit them, and sent them into the corn fields and vineyards. How bizarre is that? I can't even imagine how he could have done this. Did he build traps? Did they bite him? All I know for sure is he did it because he could, and he was angry. This destruction resulted in utter contempt and cruel retaliation on the part of the Philistines, who burned both his wife and father-in-law to death.

Naturally, Samson avenged himself with a great slaughter. We don't know the extent of this slaughter, but the Bible refers to it as vicious. I imagine it did not cease until his anger was appeased, which could have easily cost the Philistines hundreds of lives. Rather than bring risk to his parents, he went to a cave and stayed there. Would his parents ever see him again? Surely, they eventually heard of this battle, because the region was small and their son was now famous. When the utterly humiliated Philistines encamped in Lehi, where the Israelites dwelt, they gave the Israelites an offer they couldn't refuse, and the Israelites knew just where to find Samson. They coordinated an action plan to capture him and turn him over. Deep within himself, Samson did not resent the Israelites for assisting in his capture. Where did this loyalty to God and his countrymen come from? Could it have been from his devoted parents? By now Samson knew his strength. He knew what he was capable of doing. Yet he yielded.

> Then three thousand men of Judah went down to the cleft of the rock of Etam, and said to Samson, "Do you not know that the Philistines rule over us? What is this you have done to us?" And he said to them, "As they did to me, so I have done to them." But they said to him, "We

have come down to arrest you, that we may deliver you into the hand of the Philistines." Then Samson said to them, "Swear to me you will not kill me yourselves." So they spake, saying, "No, but we will tie you securely and deliver you into their hand; but we will surely not kill you." And they bound him with two new ropes and brought him up from the rock (Judges 15:11-13).

To be honest, I don't have a whole lot of respect for these men at this juncture. In order to save their own skins, they turned their hero over to these ruthless characters who would burn their own people alive. How much worse would the Philistines treat Samson, their sworn enemy? As the Philistines charged at him, the Spirit of the Lord came upon him and the cords broke loose as easily as if a child had tied them. He spotted a fresh jawbone of a donkey and slew 1,000 men with it. Have you ever tried to picture this scene? An army of Philistines equipped with swords, knives, and who knows what else against one man with a natural weapon in one hand. Can you imagine the strength and stamina required to duck quick enough and swing fast enough to kill that many trained men? No doubt, in the spirit realm Samson wasn't alone. I must say where Samson lacked in good judgment, he made up for it in resourcefulness. Now the miracles occurred rapidly in succession. Samson credited the Lord for the great deliverance then realized how thirsty he was. He crudely questioned God about His true motives (Judg. 15:15,18*)*.

Even though Samson's request was irreverent, God broke the cheek tooth on the jawbone, the tooth dead center on the bottom row, and water gushed out! Samson named that place *En Hakkore,* which means "spring or the fountain of him that prayed." God meets the needs of His people. This is similar to when Moses struck the rock in Meribah, which means "contentious," and the people were just that. They can get quite testy when dehydrated. Moses was no exception. Clearly, Samson believed from his young years all that had been taught to him and that he was God's servant. Now, like Moses, he was experiencing the rewards of a life of serving God.

When close to 20 years old he accepted a judgeship over Israel that lasted from 1075–1055 B.C. This was a time of relative peace for the nation still under the control of the Philistines. Evidently his parents' heartache, when Samson took matters into his own hands, paid off. The Israelites elected him to rule and protect them. Throughout his years, Samson exercised more discipline than not. One sentence covers 20 years of his life as a judge. While this in and of itself is not that unusual, for Samson it spelled triumph and self-control. No wrongdoings were recorded. He controlled his impulses and desires. He stayed within his very limited boundaries. Under God, his exploits were amazing. He was the twelfth of thirteen judges. Judges ruled at intervals, not necessarily in succession but oftentimes concurrently. Judges were individuals God raised up for the deliverance of His people from both themselves and their enemies.[15] Samson's leadership as judge or deliverer did not take the form of leading an army against the Philistines. Rather, it consisted of being a lone champion for the cause of his people. His exploits distracted the Philistines from more serious invasions into the tribal areas of Benjamin and Judah.[16]

Then to Samson's own undoing, he sauntered into Philistine territory—too close to the *forbidden fruit* again. As strong as he was, the temptation of a beautiful woman was too much for him. Despite his upbringing and knowledge of God's commandments, he fell victim to Satan's evil scheme as so many pastors, ministers, and priests have done. Few have had to make recompense like Samson. Maybe their exposed sins cost them their reputation, money, or even position, but never their eyesight and freedom. Upon entering Gaza, he spotted a Philistine harlot and lay with her. This was a sin of fornication and a violation of

---

15. Henry Halley, *Halley's Bible Handbook* (Minneapolis, MI: Zondervan Publishing House, 1964) 119.

16. John F. Walvoord and Roy B Zuck, *The Bible Knowledge Commentary*, (Colorado Springs, CO: David C Cook 1985), 404.

God's command to the nation not to consort with foreigners, yet he did not break his Nazirite vow.

This one act of indiscretion is marked with a stronger message from Samson. Aware of Samson's presence in the city, the Philistines of Gaza lay in wait for him all night at the city gate, planning to kill him when he left at dawn. However, Samson arose in the middle of the night, apparently catching them by surprise. He escaped by pulling up the doors of the city gate, together with the two posts, bar and all, and carried them up a mountain facing Hebron! Local tradition identifies the hill as El Montar, just east of Gaza (possibly a distance of 37 miles). There seemed to be no reason why Samson would carry the doors further, since he had already insulted the people of the city by removing its gate of security.[17] It was as if to say to the Philistines, "This is what I think of you and your incessant harassment."

Scripture speaks no more of Samson's parents or when they passed. They had one thing and one thing only to hang on to regarding their wayward and highly unpredictable son—his upbringing. They loved their son, and they made sure he knew God loved him. They went above and beyond what every parent/guardian is supposed to do. They raised him in the way of the Lord. They represented our true Father up in heaven. Once Samson left home for good, they had to rely on the seed they planted in him from birth and that God would cause the increase. They died not seeing but believing the prayers and training that they provided for their only child would bear fruit.

> Therefore you shall lay up these words of mine in your heart and in your soul, and bind them as a sign on your hand, and they shall be as frontlets between your eyes. You shall teach them to your children, speaking of them when you sit in your house, when you walk

17. John F. Walvoord and Roy B Zuck, *The Bible Knowledge Commentary*, (Colorado Springs, CO: David C Cook 1985), 407.

by the way, when you lie down, and when you rise up (Deuteronomy 11:18-19).

Train up a child in the way he should go, And when he is old he will not depart from it (Proverbs 22:6).

Having once again sauntered into Philistine territory, the Valley of Sorek, Samson met *Delilah*, a Philistine with a Semitic name that means *devotee*. It seems every time Samson went into foreign territory he got into trouble. Satan kept using the same tools—anger and women. Logically, it stands to reason—if an alcoholic, stay away from bars; if a gambler, stay away from casinos, etc. Despite his upbringing, it seems that Samson did not appreciate the strictness of a Nazirite calling. He and Delilah immediately began a brief but torrid love affair. Samson let his passion and emotions for a beautiful woman blind his judgment once again. He seemed to lose all common sense and reason. He didn't even seem to suspect her persistent nagging him for the source of his power. In true harlot fashion, Delilah accepted a deal for $5,500 from five Philistine lords to betray Samson in order to put him down and reduce him to helplessness. It took four attempts to finally succeed, or so they thought. Somebody like Samson, anointed of the Lord, could never be defeated—not in this life or the next.

Although Samson was strong willed, God could and did work with him, just as He can you. Nothing is impossible for God (Luke 1:37).

No matter how disobedient and stubborn he was, i.e. doing things his way and not the way he was taught, God used him. If God so chooses, He can and will use you for His purpose and glory. If he used Samson through his disobedience, how much more can He use you through your obedience?

Initially Delilah wanted to know two specific things: *"So Delilah said to Samson, Please tell me where your great strength lies, and with what you may be bound to afflict you"* (Judg. 16:6).

It makes you wonder why he didn't suspect her motives for wanting to know these things. He'd been around this mountain before. I started to write all sorts of theories but instead decided on the old adage: "Fool me once, shame on you; fool me twice, shame on me; fool me three times...I deserve it."

The first false answer Samson gave her was, *"If they bind me with seven fresh bowstrings, not yet dried, then I shall become weak, and be like any other man"* (Judg. 16:7). As ridiculous as this was, it was very specific, but it didn't work.

Delilah limited her next three requests to one thing—how he might be bound. He answered her in a similar way but replaced green bow-strings with new ropes instead. And he repeated, *"Then I shall be like any other man"* (Judg. 16:11). Each time he was getting closer to the whole truth.

The third deception was diluted so much an amateur could have figured it out because this time Samson brought attention to his hair. He told her she could weave his seven locks or braids into the fabric on the loom and then pin it (Judg. 16:13). Now the rope imagery was unraveling—weave his hair like bands of rope designed to keep him bound. Why seven locks? Seven is the number for completion. Maybe he was prophesying over himself, or maybe God was telling him through his own voice he was near the completion of his calling or life or both.

This was the third time Samson confessed he would become weak like any other man. He confessed weakness over himself. From this we learn going forward that we can have what we say. We must be careful what we confess because it can work against you and give Satan an advantage. See Jesus' example of what happens when we believe what we say.

> So Jesus answered and said to them, "Have faith in God. For assuredly, I say to you, whoever says to this

mountain, 'Be removed and be cast into the sea,' and does not doubt in his heart, but believes that those things he says will be done, he will have whatever he says" (Mark 11:22-23).

Samson did speak disaster over his life, but nobody deserves what was about to happen to him. Again, Delilah's pretty, petite little self pouted and demanded to have her way. She wanted proof that he really loved her—the ultimate in deception and treachery, playing on a man's heart strings. After she had stirred havoc in their relationship, he told her the truth—that if his head were to be shaved he would be weak and just like any other man. Here we see that Samson was not misnamed. He knew he was called to be a Nazirite "unto God." He just had no idea how he would fulfill this calling.

And it came to pass, when she pestered him daily with her words and pressed him, so that his soul was vexed to death, that he told her all his heart, and said to her, "No razor has ever come upon my head, for I have been a Nazirite **unto God** from my mother's womb. If I am shaven then my strength will leave me, and I shall become weak, and be like any other man" (Judges 16:16-17).

The ruthless woman who betrayed Samson's trust clearly wasn't about to give up because of the greed in her heart. It didn't matter what they did to him, she wanted her blood money. Delilah counting her silver was probably the last thing Samson saw before the Philistines scooped out his eyes. The role she played wasn't like what we have seen in Hollywood movies with a glamourous looking woman. The real Delilah is right up there with some of the most evil women in the Bible. In her effort to seal the deal, she actually had the Philistines staked out in her room witnessing while the transgressions took place. Samson's wife betrayed him out of fear; Delilah betrayed him out of greed. Her unfaithfulness to Samson brought ruin to him and to her people.[18]

As we have already seen, as a Nazirite, Samson was born into a restricted diet of no wine or strong drink, no berries from the vine, and nothing "unclean." In Jewish culture, unclean food includes an extensive list to be researched separately. Judaism also had its own set of strict rules. These were the laws, statutes, and ordinances of the Old Testament. The Jewish collection of traditions, later recognized as the Mishna, and Jewish commentaries on the traditions later called the Talmud and Gemara (authoritative collections) were gradually accepted as manmade law.

To summarize Samson's life thus far, he slept with two women outside of marriage—one for one night (the harlot from Timnah) the other for maybe a total of 30 days (Delilah from Sorek), if that. Since I doubt his marriage of barely one week was even consummated because the ceremony broke up just short of that, I cannot definitively refer to his sexual infractions as adultery. These sexual infractions were possibly 30 days out of less than 50 years of his whole life. Compared to the average man, Samson was a saint! Furthermore, there is no specific event where he imbibed in any kind of alcohol. It is assumed he did because of his consorting with these two prostitutes and especially because the Philistines shaved off his hair without waking him up. Samson never cut or shaved his own hair. The Philistines did. I believe he never once broke his God-given Nazirite vow. Despite a razor being put to his head, there is something honorable about Samson's protecting his vow.

Because the plan to strip him of his dignity and freedom had failed three times, the Philistines had to get it right this time. When Samson appeared most vincible, lulled to sleep on Delilah's lap, they hurriedly

---

18. Insert about Delilah, *New King James Version: Life Application Study Bible* (United States: Tyndale House Publishers, Incorporated, 1996), 417.

shaved the seven locks from his head and *God's presence left*. He became as weak as any other man. He was no longer a threat to the Philistines.

> And she said, "The Philistines are upon you, Samson!" So he awoke from his sleep, and said, "I will go out as before, at other times, and shake myself free!" But he did not know that the Lord had departed from him (Judges 16:20).

Then they "put out his eyes." The Hebrew word for "put" is *naqar* which means "to bore, penetrate, quarry, dig, pick out, thrust out." What can I say? God had departed from him. How ghastly! Which was worse, the ghoulish eye purge or God's departure? And it was here that Samson became a symbol of Christ to come. Each were betrayed leading to their demise. Each suffered horrific atrocities. Christ suffered many things, but it wasn't until late into His suffering that He felt mankind's sins resting on His soul: *"And at the ninth hour Jesus cried out with a loud voice, saying, 'Eloi, Eloi, lama sabachthani?' which is translated, 'My God, My God, why have you forsaken me?'"* (Mark 15:34). Each learned submission through the anguish they endured.

> Though He was a Son, yet He learned obedience by the things which He suffered (Hebrews 5:8).

Now blind and aware of the power of a broken vow, Samson was reduced to the work of an ox—fettered in heavy bronze, his whole life consisted of grinding wheat in the prison. He sightlessly and endlessly went round and round. Try to imagine some of the thoughts he may have had, the regrets he had. It was hell on earth. If only he could find one opening, one opportunity, he would jump at it. Even death would be an escape.

We don't know how long he had ox duty, but we do know his hair began to grow. Hair professionals have confirmed that an average, healthy, middle-age male grows one half inch a month or one inch every two months. I'm estimating Samson was grinding for four to six months. While his hair would only be two or three inches long, the issue never was about his hair. It was about obedience and honoring the God of his fathers. Some believe his strength was in his hair. The notion is as ridiculous as it sounds. Samson's special separation to the Lord through his Nazirite status was symbolized by his uncut hair.[19] Samson explained his Nazirite status to Delilah when he could no longer bear her nagging him for his secret. He said that if his head were shaved, he would become as weak as any other man. This was not because his strength was in his hair but because cutting it would manifest his disobedience to the Lord—disobedience that had already begun by his revealing the truth to Delilah, whom he had no reason to trust. His superhuman strength came from the power of God. When God's Spirit rested on him, no army could defeat him. What the devil meant for harm, God worked for good. No matter who said it when, the principle still remains.

> But as for you, you meant evil against me; but God meant
> it for good, in order to bring it about as it is this day, to
> save many people alive (Genesis 50:20).

The Philistines were anxious to show off their conquest with a celebration. The plan was to mock and humiliate Samson and to avenge and vindicate themselves for the humiliation they had endured at the hands of this "maniac." They put him on display in order to honor their grain deity, Dagon, and make a comedic roast out of their victory. The best part of the end of this story isn't Samson pushing two pillars apart, thus upsetting the structural integrity of the building and causing it to collapse, but his surrender to God once more. He knew he had gotten himself into this situation. He didn't blame God; he blamed himself. Before he even realized his strength had returned, he acted in faith.

19. John F. Walvoord and Roy B Zuck, *The Bible Knowledge Commentary*, (Colorado Springs, CO: David C Cook 1985), 407.

Here was his opportunity to not only escape through death the horrible life he had created for himself but to show the God of his father what he was really made of. He was a son of the living Lord God, Son, and Holy Spirit. He truly repented for his mistakes. He wanted cleansing and renewal. He longed to go to the place of his fathers, his eternal home, to his once nurturing and forgiving parents who believed in him and, out of love, pointed the way to God, his heavenly Father.

Through his supplication, the Spirit of God arrived. Now Samson, fully ensconced with power, pushed against the middle pillars with all his might and the temple fell. I estimate that there were approximately 5,000 people in the building, 3,000 of whom were elite commanders, lords and their families watching from the roof. I believe Samson took out roughly 6,530 Philistines total in his lifetime. His weapons were his hands and his ammunition was the power of God.

> And Samson called to the Lord, saying, "O Lord God, remember, I pray! Strengthen me, I pray, just this once, O God, that I may with one blow take vengeance on the Philistines for my two eyes!" And Samson took hold of the two middle pillars which supported the temple, and he braced himself against them, one on his right and the other on his left. Then Samson said, "Let me die with the Philistines!" And he pushed with all his might, and the temple fell on the lords and all the people who were in it. So the dead that he killed at his death were more than he had killed in his life (Judges 16:28-30).

Again, Samson was a symbol of Christ even in his death. Angels came directly to their mothers and foretold the special circumstances by which they would be born and the service they would render unto God. Now let's take a look at their deaths. As Christ triumphed in His death over Satan and his hosts, Samson's strength was resurrected to take out his enemies one last time.

Samson's entire family, kinsmen, and tribe traveled the 35 miles to salvage his remains. No danger is mentioned, but as with any other occupied territory there was risk involved. They took him and buried him in Manoah's tomb with his parents.

This story is not yet over. Guess who made it into the New Testament Hall of Faith? His name is mentioned with David, Samuel, the prophets, Gideon, Barak, and Jephthah all in the same sentence.

> And what more shall I say? For the time would fail me
> to tell of Gideon and Barak and Samson and Jephthah,
> also of David and Samuel and the prophets: who through
> faith subdued kingdoms, worked righteousness, obtained
> promises, stopped the mouths of lions, quenched the vio-
> lence of fire, escaped the edge of the sword, out of weak-
> ness were made strong, became valiant in battle, turned
> to flight the armies of the aliens (Hebrews 11:32-34).

These men were worthy because of the heroic feats they performed. Out of the nine listed, Samson performed six of them. He, through faith, shut the mouth of a lion, he emerged unscathed from battle, he was brave in war, he drove back foreign invaders, out of weakness was made strong, and became valiant in battle. In addition, he lived in a cave and was tortured, chained, and imprisoned yet did not receive the promise.

> And all these, having obtained a good testimony through
> faith, did not receive the promise, God having provided
> something better for us, that they should not be made
> perfect apart from us (Hebrews 11:39-40).

These people were the precursors to the greatness that succeeded them in the New Testament—the body of Christ, both messianic and Gentile—you and me. Falling away is one thing; coming back, returning to your Creator, is quite another. In this regard, Samson fit beautifully

68

into the Hall of Faith. We, too, are in the Hall of Faith under "us." Scripture says we will be perfected when we are with Him. "Him" who? Jesus, of course.

> But ye are come unto mount Sion, and unto the city of the living God, the heavenly Jerusalem, and to an innumerable company of angels, To the general assembly and church of the first born, which are written in heaven, and God the Judge of all, and to the spirits of just men made perfect (Hebrews 12:22-23).

Who told Samson about God, what it meant to be a Nazirite, the role of the angels, their visitation, etc.? Naturally we assume it was his parents who loved him and stood by him until the end of their days. Who first told you? Whom have you told? Greatness in the eyes of God is your faithfulness to Him. There may be one Hall of Faith recorded in the Bible, but there is the Book of Life recorded eternally in heaven. Believe in and serve with all your heart the God who created you, who died for you, and you too will gain entry into heaven's Hall of Faith.

> Rejoice that your names are written in heaven (Luke 10:20b).

Chapter Four

The Betrayal of Absalom: David
and Absalom

What a mess! Who would have thought such a complex infusion of raw lust and love could spawn from Israel's most famous family? The thread of Absalom's betrayal weaved throughout this story shines a bright light on God's love and ability to restore. Let's find out how.

Early on, while staying in Gath with a Philistine king named Achish to escape capture from King Saul of Israel, David covertly raided several towns, thus slowly wiping out the enemies of Israel. It is believed David found and took his wife Maacah while performing a "savage raid upon Geshur." She bore him Absalom and Tamar.[20] Absalom was the third of six sons born to King David in Hebron, a mid-western section of Judea, where he reigned for seven and a half years. Absalom was the son of Maacah, daughter of Talmai, son of Ammihud, King of Geshur, which is in Syria.

Years later, David's firstborn son Amnon, born of Ahinoam of Jezreel, *loved* Absalom's sister, Tamar, so much that he had to have her. The

---

20. Footnote from 2 Samuel 13:37, *The Old ScofieldRG Study Bible*, KJV, Standard Edition (United States: Oxford University Press, 1996), 369.

71

Hebrew word used for "love" is *ahab,* which means "to have an affection for." Catching a glimpse of familiarity here? Wait for it. It wasn't enough that Amnon lusted after his half-sister, but he used his father David to get Tamar to go to his house where he could be alone with her.

> Then Amnon lay down and pretended to be ill; and when the king came to see him, Amnon said to the king, "Please let Tamar my sister come and make a couple of cakes in my sight, that I may eat from her hand." And David sent home to Tamar, saying, "Now go to your brother Amnon's house, and prepare food for him." So, Tamar went to her brother Amnon's house; and he was lying down (2 Samuel 13:6-8).

Amnon forced himself on her then kicked her to the curb. Let's look at that for a minute. Having worked with sex offenders in the second decade of my career, I can attest to the fact that rape usually does not occur because of infatuation or lasciviousness. There is often an underlying motive for such a violent act. Rape stems from pent-up rage. We can't ignore how Amnon went from "loving" her to hating her within minutes. He was extremely cruel in his dealings with her.

> Then Amnon was seized with extreme hatred for her; the hatred he now felt for her was greater than his earlier love. "Get up and go," he said. "No, my brother, she said, "to send me away would be a greater wrong than the other you have done to me." But he would not listen to her. He called the soldier who was his servant. "Get rid of this woman for me," he said, "throw her out and bolt the door after her." So, the servant put her out and bolted the door after her (2 Samuel 13:15-18b).

There is no talk of Amnon ever having raped again during the next two years. All we know for sure is that his attack on Tamar was a violent and cruel act that resulted in deadly recompense for him and negatively impacted a whole country. Tamar stayed with her brother Absalom for two years, desolate and living in shame. Absalom's hatred for Amnon grew so much that he successfully arranged to have his servants kill him.

Strangely, Absalom also made David complicit in Amnon's death.

> Two years later, when Absalom's sheep shearers were at Baal Hazor near the border of Ephraim, he invited all the king's sons to come there. Absalom went to the king and said, "Your servant has had shearers come. Will the king and his officials please join me?" "No, my son," the king replied. "All of us should not go; we would only be a burden to you." Although Absalom urged him, he still refused to go, but gave him his blessing. Then Absalom said, "If not, please let my brother Amnon come with us." The king asked him, "Why should he go with you?" But Absalom urged him, so he sent with him Amnon and the rest of the king's sons (2 Samuel 13:23-27).

Here, the plot gets sludge thick when Absalom carries out his plan of revenge. One has to ask, didn't it matter at all that his father, the king, would disapprove? Clearly, if David didn't exact a punishment on Amnon, he would never permit his demise to be contracted by one of his own sons no less. And how did David never once hear about or suspect Absalom's plot?

It made me wonder how "in the know" David really was when it came to his own immediate family. It also makes me wonder how "in the know" we are when it comes to our immediate family. Absalom may have been the most handsome in all of Israel, but somehow he opened a door to Satan's evil spirits. So Absalom murdered Amnon, yet it took David longer to get over Absalom's three-year absconding to Geshur than for him to get over Amnon's murder.

But Absalom fled, and went to Talmai [his grandfather], the son of Ammihud, the king of Geshur, and David mourned for his son every day. So, Absalom fled, and went to Geshur, and was there three years. And the soul of King David was consumed with or longed to go forth unto his son Absalom; for he was comforted concerning Amnon, seeing he was dead" (2 Samuel 13:37-39).

This too has a familiar ring. Why? Let's back up a second.

Most people know the story of David and Bathsheba. Bathsheba was married to a great and loyal soldier whose name was Uriah, the Hittite. Uriah was fighting with the Israelites who had just captured Ammon (not to be confused with David's son Amnon) and about to surround its chief city, Rabbah. One night while walking around the palace roof, David spotted this beautiful woman bathing on her rooftop below. He wanted to know her better, including in the biblical sense, and had her brought to him. Soon she became with child. Adding to the intrigue, David sent for Uriah under the pretense of wanting to know how the war was going. Despite David's efforts, which included getting him drunk two nights in a row to get Uriah to go home and be with his wife, Uriah's loyalty to the Ark of God, his king, his commander, his fellow soldiers, and his country would not allow him to enjoy the pleasures of marriage. Hence, Uriah was instructed by David to carry a personal note to Joab, the king's commander, ordering Uriah to the front lines while the rest of the Israeli fighters were to draw back. Unknowingly, Uriah had a part to play in his own demise. This greatly displeased the Lord, so He sent the prophet Nathan to King David. Please note, three separate times we see the characters in this story scheming to involve others to carry out their impious plan. David was involved each time.

Nathan promptly rebuked David via a parable that opened David's eyes to the sin he committed. Nathan then prophesied that the sword and calamity would never leave his household. He would lose the son born between himself and Bathsheba. David spent one week of the unnamed baby's life pleading, fasting, and praying prostrate on the ground, expressing his grief and despair (2 Sam. 12:13-23). Upon learning he died, strangely, David returned instantly to a normal life. The next few verses describe David's bizarre response to his son's passing:

> He answered, while the child was alive, I fasted and wept, I thought, 'Who knows? The Lord may be gracious to me and let the child live.' But now that he is dead why should I fast? Can I bring him back again? I will go to him, but he will not return to me" (2 Samuel 12:22-23).

Can you imagine your son raping your daughter then a second son plotting murder to avenge his sister, including you as a part of his nefarious plan? Let's get real. Maybe you know of someone who has sexual abuse hidden in their family. One of the five things mentioned would be devastating enough: your son raping your daughter. Your son implicating you in the act. Another son ordering his demise. That son implicating you in the act. Your innocent daughter humbled to isolation, shame, and rejection. For the sake of space, let's examine the fifth one. Tamar was obviously much loved and revered by her family as demonstrated by the beautiful coat of many colors bestowed upon her by the king (2 Sam. 13:18). Now, in her mind, she was nothing more than a horror, outcast, unloved, and most certainly unwanted. Even if she overcame this wrong thinking, there is the stigma, after years of intense therapy and prayer, of people not accepting you or looking at you the same way. This is all primarily due to ignorance. It takes a strong and very determined believer with lots of support and faith to overcome such atrocities. Fast forward...

Joab, the commander of King David's army, realized David's depth of sadness and how much he favored Absalom.[21] Therefore, he arranged to have Absalom return to Jerusalem.

---

21. Footnote from 2 Sam 14:1, *1599 Geneva Bible—Patriot's Edition* (Powder Springs, GA: Tolle Lege Press and White Hall Press, 2012), 35.

> Now Joab the son of Zeruiah perceived that the king's
> heart was toward Absalom (2 Samuel 14:1).

Evidently, Absalom's heart was not toward his father, King David
(2 Sam. 14:23-24).

I believe David considered this to be an appropriate response, i.e.
sending a signal of disapproval for Absalom's previous actions. It can
only be speculated why Absalom's feelings had soured so much after
his return home that he embarked on another sinister plan after killing
his brother. Was it due to a lack of justice for his sister Tamar? Was it
because David refused to see him upon his return? Either way, in car-
rying out this murder, he opened a door to the real enemy of old, Satan,
to fill his bitter soul with blinding hatred toward his unsuspecting father
and ultimately fulfill Nathan's prophecy.

Coming back to Jerusalem was not enough for Absalom. He took
matters into his own hands. After two years of having still not seen his
father despite two failed attempts to make arrangements through Joab,
he had his servants burn Joab's barley field. This action got Joab's attention who finally secured a meeting with the king relaying Absalom's
message that if the king wouldn't receive him he should have stayed in
Geshur. He really forced the king's hand by adding, "If I am guilty, then
let him put me to death" (2 Sam. 14:32). Upon hearing this, the king,
having mourned for his son every day, upon seeing his son for the first
time in five years, warmly welcomed him.

> Joab went to the king and told him this. He then summoned
> Absalom who went to the king and bowed low before him,
> throwing himself on his face to the ground before the king.
> And the king kissed Absalom (2 Samuel 14:33).

A token of forgiveness? Love and forgiveness go together like wet
and water. One is characteristic of the other, meaning you can't have
one without the other. How can we be sure this wasn't just a customary

greeting for that region of the world? The Hebrew word used for "kiss" here is *nashaq,* which means "to touch, burn, kindle; a sign of affection." This goes far beyond a simple salutation. Rather than David refusing to see Absalom's face, this time he responded with a *kiss* of deep, burning affection.

However, this kiss was not enough to unite the distraught hearts of father and son. Absalom, as recorded in 2 Samuel 15, began his fatal journey of treason and subterfuge. First, he stole the hearts of Israel by pretending to care about the people's problems while acting as a kind of judge at Israel's gate. Then he manipulated his father under the pretense of paying a vow to the Lord in Hebron, should he ever return to Jerusalem. Implicating his father once again, Absalom got David's permission to go back to Hebron, not realizing his son had a dual purpose to both perform sacrifices and to establish kingship. Once out of Jerusalem, Absalom deceptively gathered up 200 men, including one of David's counselors, Ahithophel, the Gilonite.

> And after four years Absalom said to the king, Pray, let me go to Hebron (his birthplace) and pay my vow to the Lord. For your servant vowed while I dwelt at Geshur in Syria, If the Lord will bring me again to Jerusalem, then I will serve the Lord (by offering a sacrifice). And the king said to him, Go in peace. So he arose, and went to Hebron. But Absalom sent secret messengers throughout all the tribes of Israel, saying, As soon as you hear the sound of the trumpet, then say, Absalom is king at Hebron. With Absalom went 200 men from Jerusalem, who were invited (as guests to his sacrificial feast); and they went in their simplicity, and they knew not a thing. And while Absalom was offering the sacrifices, he sent for Ahithophel the Gilonite, David's counselor from his city Giloh. And the conspiracy was strong; the people with Absalom increased continually (2 Samuel 15:7-12).

All during this time, David's leadership was compromised because of his incredulous sorrow over what was happening between himself and Absalom. Rather than stand and fight, David chose to withdraw from his beloved Jerusalem and not engage the country in his personal problems.

> And there came a messenger to David, saying, The hearts of the men of Israel have gone after Absalom. David said to all his servants that were with him at Jerusalem, Arise, and let us flee; or else none of us will escape from Absalom. Make haste to depart, lest he overtake us suddenly, and bring evil upon us and smite the city with the sword (2 Samuel 15:13-14).

Although David split up his troops, they all shared one thing in common—they wept (2 Sam. 15:23).

> And David went up over the Mount of Olives, and wept as he went, barefoot and his head covered. And all the people who were with him covered their heads, weeping as they went (2 Samuel 15:30).

David considered Absalom's betrayal an affliction or *oniy*—"depression, misery, trouble, tears of my eye." This affected him deeply.

Absalom's malignant ambition included the unthinkable—laying with ten of King David's concubines left behind to maintain the house, a symbolic act of rebellion.

> And Ahithophel said unto Absalom, Go in unto thy father's concubines, which he hath left to keep the house; and all Israel shall hear that thou art abhorred of thy father: then shall the hands of all that are with thee be strong. So they spread Absalom a tent upon the top of the

house; and Absalom went in unto his father's concubines in the sight of all Israel (2 Samuel 16:21-22).

In addition, Ahithophel offered to pursue David with 12,000 men ensuring Absalom that his weak and tired father would be met with certain defeat. Absalom readily agreed to this plan. Ahithophel said to Absalom,

> I would strike him with terror, and then all the people with him will flee. I would strike down only the king and bring back all the people to you. The death of the man you seek will mean the return of all; all the people will be unharmed. This plan seemed good to Absalom and to all the elders of Israel (2 Samuel 17:2b-4).

Then David was told Ahithophel, his most prized counselor, had defected to Absalom. They believed listening to Ahithophel was like listening to God himself.[22]

As David got word of Absalom's plan, David prayed for God's intervention. Sometimes God chooses to answer quickly. Whether He does or does not, we must remember that God is always faithful and right on time. God's answer was waiting for him at the top of the mountain. No sooner had David arrived than he ran into Hushai, the Archite, his friend. Together they devised a plan to plant his friend among the priests, advising contrary to Ahithophel's advice to Absalom.

> When David came to the summit (of Olivet), where he worshiped God, behold, Hushai the Archite came to meet him with his coat rent, and earth upon his head. David said to him, If you go with me, you will be a burden to me; But if you return to the city, and say to

22. Footnote from 2 Samuel 15:31, William Smith, *Smith's Bible Dictionary Complete Concordance Revised Ed.* (Nashville, TN: Holman Bible Publishers, 1991) 375.

Absalom, I will be your servant, O king; as I have been
your father's servant in the past, so will I be your servant now; then you may defeat for me the counsel of
Ahithophel (2 Samuel 15:32-34).

Then David chose three captains of might and valor, each strate-
gically placed with specific instructions to deal gently with Absalom
for the king's sake. Despite Absalom finding pleasure in both Ahithophel's plan to strike terror in King David and Hushai's (false) plan to
destroy him and all the soldiers with him, Absalom preferred Hushai's
plan. Upon learning his counsel was rejected, Ahithophel went home
and killed himself.

Absalom and all the men of Israel said, "The advice of
Hushai the Archite is better than that of Ahithophel." For
the Lord had determined to frustrate the good advice of
Ahithophel in order to bring disaster on Absalom. When
Ahithophel saw that his advice had not been followed,
he saddled his donkey and headed out for his house in
his hometown. He put his house in order then hanged
himself. So he died and was buried in his father's tomb
(2 Samuel 17:14, 23).

When we seek God, like David did, God intervenes in our lives even
down to the minutest detail. We can count on Him.

And David numbered the people that were with him, and set
captains of thousands and captains of hundreds over them.
And the king commanded Joab and Abishai and Ittai, saying, Deal gently for my sake with the young man, even with
Absalom. And all the people heard when the king gave all
the captains charge concerning Absalom (2 Samuel 18:1,5).

After a great slaughter of 20,000 Israelites resulting in a huge victory for David, his only concern was for his son.

I want to make known the hideous and cowardly death perpetrated upon the young man Absalom against the will of King David. The point here is not that Joab took control of a pathetic situation, but what Absalom sowed unto himself. Joab's story, which doesn't end well for him, can be found in 1 Kings 2.

> God will not be mocked; what things you sow you shall also reap (Galatians 6:7).

> He that leadeth into captivity shall go into captivity: he that killeth by the sword must be killed by the sword. Here is the patience and the faith of the saints (Revelation 13:10).

He who lives by the sword shall die by the sword.

> Now Absalom met the servants of David, And Absalom rode upon a mule, and the mule came under a great thick oak: and his head caught hold of the oak, and he was taken up between the heaven and the earth: and the mule that was under him went away (2 Samuel 18:9).

Why do I say Absalom's death was cowardly? There he hung under an oak tree, defenseless. His thick, heavy hair got caught up in a limb while the mule he was riding continued on.

"This is a terrible example of God's vengeance against them that are rebels or disobedient to their parents."[23] Joab arrived after learning of Absalom's plight and proceeded to throw three javelins into his heart. Absalom was still not dead, so ten of Joab's armor bearers sur-

---

23. Footnote from 2 Samuel 18:9, *1599 Geneva Bible—Patriot's Edition* (Powder Springs, GA: Tolle Lege Press and White Hall Press, 2012), lix49).

rounded him and struck him (2 Sam. 18:14-15). What can we glean from this? Take steps to remove all hatred and malice from your heart. Give Satan no place, no opening to turn an injustice back on you. But always remember God is in charge. He and He alone determines the final outcome. God turned Absalom's vain glory into shame.[24]

As was the custom, runners would be sent from the battlefield to inform the king of the progress or the outcome of the battle. The first runner, Ahimaaz, delivered a message of victory. David's only question was, "Is the young man Absalom safe?" Ahimaaz feigned ignorance. Then the second runner, Cushi, excitedly announced how the Lord avenged David and all those who rose against him. David's only question was, "Is the young man Absalom safe?"

> And Ahimaaz called, and said unto the king, "All is well." And he fell down to the earth upon his face before the king, and said, blessed be the Lord thy God, which hath delivered up the men that lifted up their hand against my lord the king. And the king said, "Is the young man Absalom safe?" And Ahimaaz answered, "When Joab sent the king's servant, and me thy servant, I saw a great tumult, but I knew not what it was." ... And, behold, Cushi came; and Cushi said, "Tidings, my lord the king: for the Lord hath avenged thee this day of all them that rose up against thee." And the king said unto Cushi, Is the young man Absalom safe? And Cushi answered, "The enemies of my lord the king, and all that rise against thee to do thee hurt, be as that young man is" (2 Samuel 18:28-32).

When told that Absalom had been killed, David was so deeply heartbroken he got alone and wept, saying, "O my son Absalom, my son, my

---

24. Footnote from 2 Samuel 18:17, *1599 Geneva Bible—Patriot's Edition* (Powder Springs, GA: Tolle Lege Press and White Hall Press, 2012), xlix50.

son Absalom! Would God I had died for thee, O Absalom, my son, my son!" (2 Sam. 18:33).

David's grief was so deep that it moved all of Israel. Victory was turned into mourning for the people. They stole away in shame as David cried over and over, "O my son Absalom!" Imagine a king of David's magnitude wailing for all to see that the enemy, whom they thought they had defeated, was in fact the desire of David's heart. The victory they sought so hard to achieve resulted in crushing their leader, decimating him to tears at his son's death. He shifted Absalom's defeat to himself, wishing it were him that died rather than his own flesh and blood. His love culminated in unbearable pain knowing Absalom died hating him.

What is the lesson to be learned here? Jesus experiences pain and rejection every time we sin. In essence, we are rebelling when we purposefully disobey Him. He loves us more than David loved Absalom. Are we going to continue chasing sin like Absalom chased David, or are we going to surrender to God, who is willing to shower us with mercy and forgiveness even to the bitter end? David didn't seem to get bitter. He mourned and grieved but didn't allow his sorrow to become hate-filled or vengeful. Satan could not change his heart because it belonged to God.

> And when He [God] had removed him [Saul], He raised up for them David as king, to whom also He gave testimony and said, 'I have found David, the son of Jesse, a man after my own heart, who will do all My will.' From this man's seed, according to the promise, God raised up for Israel a Savior—Jesus (Acts 13:22-23).

The only question that remains is, "Did anything good come of the relationship between David and Absalom?" David mourned for Absalom to his dying day, unlike the seven-day-old child he had with Bathsheba or his oldest son Amnon. What kind of love could make his heart burn in sorrow through the years of great success and centuries of renown? I can only think of one kind—the *love* God has for us. This self-sacrificial, deep, lasting, kind, charitable, merciful, reaffirming, and sometimes painful but always unconditional love is known as *agape*. Through David, we see a type of the persistent and endless love our heavenly Father and Lord Jesus Christ have for all of us.

Chapter Five

To Love and Not Be Loved in Return: Hosea and Gomer

G od's unchanging love, forgiveness, and perseverance in the face of our human condition and propensity for sin is best illustrated by Hosea's love for Gomer. Overshadowed by a much bigger picture of God's love for Israel, the parallel between the two relationships was God's draw to His beloved nation to come back to Him.

Both God and Hosea knew the choice their beloveds would make, i.e., the house of Israel and Gomer would commit adultery. Hosea's marriage to an unfaithful woman would emulate God's relationship with the unfaithful nation of Israel. I want to stop here and remind every reader that God has never given up on Israel and will never give up on us. No matter what our sin, God's love triumphs. Don't give up on yourself.

Hosea, which means "salvation," became a prophet in Israel for 38 years in 753 B.C. under Jeroboam II. God called him to marry someone he knew would be unfaithful, i.e. "a wife of harlotry" or "a wife of whoredom" who would hurt him deeply.

> When the Lord began to speak through Hosea, the
> Lord said to him, "Go, take to yourself an adulterous

85

wife and children of unfaithfulness, because the land is guilty of the vilest adultery in departing from the Lord" (Hosea 1:2).

Now, if God wanted Hosea to do this, it stands to reason God was revealing Himself through this prophet. Hosea unveils God's infinite love and ability to feel pain.

> For we do not have a high priest who is unable to sympathize with our weaknesses, but we have one who has been tempted in every way, just as we are, yet without sin (Hebrews 4:15).

Think about this assignment. Hosea was to spend the rest of his life with a woman who would not only cheat on him but have offspring by the men she cheated with!

Hosea and Gomer had a male child they named *Jezreel*, which means "God will sow." Hosea's pain began when the second and again third child were born to Gomer. There is every reason to believe that these two children were born from infidelity. The biggest clues were the God-given names to each child, *Lo-Ruhameh* ("no mercy") and *Lo-Ammi* ("not My people").

> Gomer conceived again and gave birth to a daughter. Then the Lord said to Hosea, "Call her Lo-Ruhamah, for I will no longer show love to the house of Israel, that I should at all forgive them. After she had weaned Lo-Ruhamah, Gomer had another son. Then the Lord said, "Call him Lo-Ammi, for you are not my people, and I am not your God" (Hosea 1:6, 8-9).

Yet God did not leave His people without hope. Throughout Hosea's ministry, the nation of Israel was reminded that a day of restoration would come when they once again would be called sons of the living God.

> Yet the number of the children of Israel shall be as the sand of the sea, which cannot be measured or numbered; and it shall come to pass, that in the place where it was said unto them, Ye are not my people, there it shall be said unto them, Ye are the sons of the living God (Hosea 1:10).

The story goes on to speak of Israel's unfaithfulness toward God. Many warnings notwithstanding, Israel attempted to forge an alliance with Assyria and Egypt.

> Ephraim (Israel) also is like a silly dove without heart: they call to Egypt, they go to Assyria (Hosea 7:11).

> He (Ephraim) makes a treaty with Assyria and sends olive oil to Egypt (Hosea 12:1b).

If that wasn't enough, they combined the idol worship from these nations with their own.

> Because Ephraim hath made many altars to sin, altars shall be unto him to sin. They sacrifice flesh for the sacrifices of mine offerings, and eat it; but the Lord accepteth them not; now will he remember their iniquity, and visit their sins; they shall return to Egypt (Hosea 8:11,13).

> And now they sin more and more, and have made them molten images of their silver, and idols according to their own understanding, all of it the work of the craftsmen: they say of them, Let the men that sacrifice kiss

the calves. Yet I am the Lord thy God from the land of Egypt, and thou shalt know no god but me: for there is no savior beside me (Hosea 13:2,4 KJV).

As a result of their idolatry, northern Israel and Judah were rejected by God for a season and went into exile.

My God will cast them away, because they did not hearken unto him: and they shall be wanderers among the nations (Hosea 9:17 KJV).

But God gave them a way out—Himself.

O Israel, return to the Lord your God, For you have stumbled because of your iniquity; Take words with you, and return to the Lord, Say to Him, "Take away all iniquity; Receive us graciously, For we will offer the sacrifices of our lips. I will heal their backsliding, I will love them freely, For My anger has been turned away from Him." Who is wise? Let him understand these things. Who is prudent? Let him know them. For the ways of the Lord are right; The righteous walk in them, but transgressors stumble in them (Hosea 14:1-2,4,9).

Through repentance, God forgave them. Once we see the destructiveness of sin and the futility of life without God, we begin to lean on His mercy. We can be confident that we have received it because God is gracious and loving and wants to restore us to Himself, just as He wanted to restore Israel. God's mercies never fail.[25]

Meanwhile, things weren't going so peachy for Hosea either. He had every reason to be finished with Gomer once and for all. Evidently, she no longer resided with him and Jezreel, their firstborn son. Good

---

25. Footnote from Hosea 14:1-2, *New King James Version: Life Application Study Bible* (United States: Tyndale House Publishers, Incorporated, 1996), 1543.

riddance. Despite knowing this would happen, it was no doubt very painful and humiliating. Being cheated on is one of the worst feelings in the world. You feel violated. It is a violation of your trust. You feel guilty. You go over every detail of your relationship trying to figure out what you did wrong. You conjure up images of what it must have been like between your ex and the other girl/guy. Satan gets a real foothold and throws every possible dagger at you, usually ending with depression or worse.

It is interesting to note that in Hosea 2:2, God wanted Hosea to *plead* with Gomer. "Plead with your mother (your nation); plead, for she is not My wife, and I am not her husband; plead that she put away her (marks of) harlotry from her face and her adulteries from between her breasts." The Hebrew word for "plead" is *ruwb*, which means to "grapple, wrangle, or strive." This illustrates God's intense pursuit to save His nation and ultimately the world. We refer to those who willingly come out of the world as the remnant. He loves the remnant, or those who shall be heirs of salvation, so much that He would risk pain and humiliation to win them to Himself.

> Looking unto Jesus the author and finisher of our faith; who for the joy that was set before Him endured the cross, despising the shame, and is set down at the right hand of the throne of God (Hebrews 12:2).

We have seen this kind of love before—*agape* love. The kind of love that rips your heart out. The kind of love where one would jump in front of a car to protect you.

> I am the good shepherd. The good shepherd gives His life for the sheep. As the Father knows Me, even so I know the Father, and I lay down my life for the sheep (John 10:11,15).

By this we know love, because He laid down His life for us. And we also ought to lay down our lives for the brethren (1 John 3:16).

The Lord goes on to say He will *allure* Israel. The Hebrew word for "allure" is *pathah,* which means to "entice or persuade." God will woo her with tender words, endear her with promises of righteousness, justice, steadfast love, and mercy.

Therefore, I will go to her and I will allure her; I will lead her in the desert and speak tenderly to her. "And in that day," declares the Lord, "you will call me 'my husband'; you will no longer call me 'my master.' And I will betroth you to Me forever; I will betroth you in righteousness and justice, in love and compassion. I will betroth you to me in faithfulness, and you will acknowledge the Lord" (Hosea 2:14,16,19-20).

Israel would no longer be slaves but united in an everlasting relationship with their one true God. Who wouldn't want these things?

First He courts us, then He freely and mercifully offers us eternal life by grace through the blood sacrifice of Jesus Christ. Without this sacrifice, we must pay for our own sins through eternal incarceration in hell. "God was promising a fresh new beginning. God's wedding gift to His people, both in Hosea's day and in our own, is His mercy. Through no merit of our own God forgives us and makes us right with Him. There is no way for us by our own efforts to reach God's high standards for a moral and spiritual life, but He graciously accepts us, forgives us, and draws us into a relationship with Himself." In that relationship we have personal and intimate communion with Him.[26] Even in the New Testament it is said:

---

26. Footnote from Hosea 2: 19-20, *New King James Version: Life Application Study Bible* (United States: Tyndale House Publishers, Incorporated, 1996), 1526.

> Once you were not a people (at all), but now you are
> God's people; once you were unpitied, but now you are
> pitied and have received mercy (1 Peter 2:10).

Even the elements get involved.

> And in that day, I will respond, says the Lord; I will
> respond to the heavens [which ask for rain to pour on the
> earth], and they shall respond to the earth [which begs for
> the rain it needs]; And the earth shall respond to the grain
> and the wine and the oil [which beseech it to bring them
> forth], and these shall respond to Jezreel [restored Israel,
> who prays for a supply of them] (Hosea 2:21-22 AMPC).

God, however, had different plans for Hosea. Through him, God
would show Israel His love and *mercy*. The Hebrew word for "mercy"
is *racham,* which means "to have compassion." Then He commanded
Hosea to take his adulterous wife back all over again.

> Yahweh said to me, "Go a second time, give your love
> to a woman loved by a husband, loved by an adulteress
> in spite of it, just as Yahweh gives his love to the sons
> of Israel though they turn to other gods and love raisin
> cakes" (Hosea 3:1).

The Amplified Bible reads that Hosea returned specifically to Gomer.

> Then said the Lord to me, Go again, love [the same]
> woman [Gomer] who is beloved of a paramour and is
> an adulteress, even as the Lord loves the children of
> Israel, though they turn to other gods and love cakes
> of raisins [used in the sacrificial feasts in idol worship]
> (Hosea 3:1 AMPC).

Allow me to give you a reference to the "raisin cakes." The revered David, king of Israel 257 years before King Jeroboam's II declining reign when Hosea was called to be a prophet, chose to celebrate the return of the Ark of the Lord from the house of Obed-Edom to the city of David with both burnt offerings and fellowship offerings. Then he blessed the people and gave each man and woman a generous piece of meat, a loaf of bread, and a cake of raisins before returning to their homes (2 Sam. 6:17-19). Unfortunately, this tradition got twisted and became part of the sacrificial feast offered by pagan worshipers to idols. Too often, the Jews were influenced by neighboring countries and copied their traditions.

Just prior to this, we see that Gomer was very materialistic.

> [Gomer/Israel] said, I will go after my lovers that give me my food and my water, my wool and my flax, my oil and my refreshing drinks. And she shall follow after her lovers, but she shall not overtake them; and she shall seek them, inquiring for and requiring them, but shall not find them. Then shall she say, Let me go and return to my first husband, for then it was better with me than now (Hosea 2:5b,7).

So Hosea was to love the same adulterous, conniving, selfish, unfaithful, unrepentant woman—who didn't even love him—all over again. How emotionally unthinkable is that? Which ministry would be harder for you—this one, or building an ark for 75 years in the middle of the desert while everyone mocked you (Noah); or building a Tabernacle exactly like the one in heaven with little or no carpentry experience (Moses); or preaching to an enemy nation to save them from certain judgment (Jonah); or lying on your left side for 390 days bearing the iniquity of Israel, then turning on your right side bearing the iniquity of Judah, all the while cooking your food with cow dung and preaching destruction until it came to pass 41 years later (Ezekiel); or writing letters to the churches while chained to Roman soldiers in a filthy, dank dungeon (Paul) to name a few?

Before I was saved, I remember thinking how I hoped I was saved. I was living in sin but believed in God. I remember taking a walk and thinking, *This year, physically, I will get my teeth fixed; mentally, I will graduate with an M.Ed.; spiritually, I am dead.* I had no clue as to how to really get saved. I believed in God, but somehow I knew that was not enough. It is not enough to say you believe.

> You believe that there is one God; you do well. The demons also believe and tremble (James 2:19).

There has to be commitment. Many people think they're going to be okay because they believe in God, and compared to many they are pretty good people. God is holy and will not be around sin; therefore, the blood of Jesus, which is both holy and pure, will cleanse us from all sin.

> If we confess our sins, He is faithful and just to forgive us our sins and to cleanse us from all unrighteousness (1 John 1:9).

The only difference between a saved sinner and an unsaved sinner is that saved sinners know they are sinners and are deserving of hell. They need a Savior—Jesus, God in the flesh—who never sinned yet died in their stead.

What did God hope to accomplish by having Hosea buy or redeem Gomer? He bought her back and loved her all over again. Instead of any woman, Hosea bought Gomer back for 15 shekels of silver and one and a half homers of barley—approximately $300 and 129 gallons of barley (Hos. 3:2).

"But he (Hosea) loved her just as God loved Israel. No matter how low we sink, God is willing to buy us back—to redeem us—and to lift us up again."[27] This is a beautiful display of Christ's redemption for us on the cross. If Hosea chose someone else it would be the same as God abandoning His beloved Israel to seek a different country in which to portray His matchless mercy. That would be a contradiction in terms. God couldn't leave the nation divided and spread all over the Middle East. He was determined from the beginning to have a nation He could call His own. That nation is Israel.

> Blessed—happy, fortunate (to be envied)—is the nation whose God is the Lord, the people He has chosen as His heritage (Psalms 33:12).

The entire world needs a place to look to and see the God who loves and protects His people against all odds. It is no coincidence that Israel is directly in the center of the world map, completely surrounded by enemy nations, yet maintains her sovereignty and has the most sought-after real estate in the world.

Let's pull this into our world and consider all the good things that may come our way. While writing this particular chapter, my instructor, author Gwen Moliert had to cancel. Yes, I was disappointed, but I prayed for her and moved on. Remember, all good things come from above.

> Every good gift and every perfect gift is from above, and comes down from the Father of lights, with whom there is no variation or shadow of turning (James 1:17).

The next day, I went to the car dealership to see why my car was literally raining on the inside. Turns out the sunroof, which I hadn't used in four years, was filled to capacity and overflowing. Consequently, the water spilled down through the ceiling, along the steel, into my interior electronics, then to the floor, which became saturated in a very short

27. Footnote from Hosea 3:2, *New King James Version: Life Application Study Bible* (United States: Tyndale House Publishers, Incorporated, 1996), 1527

amount of time with mold. Had I driven the 50-plus miles to Gwen's, I would have been breathing in all that mold. More blessings came that day. The dealership cleaned the car for free. I went to a different dealership under the umbrella of Nissan and found my friend from four years past who happened to be the sales manager. He managed to get me a trade along with some other incentives, totaling a 50 percent discount for my new (leftover) car. Did I mention the night before I had no clue as to what I would get should the car be totaled? (I could see mold creeping up the left side wall.) I said a little prayer and thought I would return to the show I was watching on TV. Instead, another commercial came on for a car I never heard of. Less than 12 hours later, I was in the showroom where my next car was waiting. Coincidence? No way!

Now how many blessings was that? I suggest tomorrow you count all of the good things that happen to you. These come from God. If you say nothing good happened, look closer. If you are saved, not one day will pass that your heavenly Father won't bless you in some way. You might ask, how do I get saved?

If you have read this far and don't know whether you are saved, I'm delighted to share with you the simple invitation for Jesus to come into your heart. Ask Him to forgive your sins and be your personal Lord and Savior.

> If you confess with your mouth the Lord Jesus and believe in your heart that God has raised Him from the dead, you will be saved. For with the heart one believes unto righteousness, and with the mouth confession is made unto salvation. For "Whoever calls on the name of the Lord shall be saved" (Romans 10:9-10,13).

If you want to know this badly, you are ready. "Whoever calls" includes all creeds, nations, and tongues. So everyone who desires to be saved can be.

We saw that Hosea "redeemed" Gomer. He bought her with 15 shekels and one and a half homers of barley. Jesus bought you too. Not with money or silver or food but with the rarest and most precious commodity in all of existence—His blood. It is no coincidence that you are reading this. God is speaking directly to your heart.

We see that Hosea became firm with Gomer in order to accurately represent God's treatment of Israel.

> [Hosea] said to her, "For many days you must keep yourself quietly for me, not playing the whore or offering yourself to others; and I will do the same for you. For the sons of Israel will be kept for many days without a king, without a leader, without sacrifice or sacred stone, without ephod or teraphim" (Hosea 3:3-4).[28]

The Amplified Bible brings it in even closer.

> So will I also be to you (until you have proved your loyalty to me and our marital relations may be resumed) (Hosea 3:3b).

There would remain a separation until she proved worthy by being loyal and faithful. The people must realize who the real Savior is and choose Him and Him only. Once the children of Israel forsake their idolatrous ways and seek the Lord, He will receive them all over again. The nation of Israel, since the very beginning, has been the chosen people to represent the entire world. The words spoken to them also apply to us. God spoke to them firmly as He does to us, for our own good. "They (Israel) were acting like Gomer, and yet God still loved them! The people

---

28. *The Jerusalem Bible, Reader's Edition,* (Garden City, NY: Double Day and Company Inc., 1968), 1260.

had heard God's words many times, but they felt the impact of those words when they saw them acted out in Hosea's troubled home life."[29]

Israel also knew God's command to Hosea to show compassion and forgiveness to an adulterous wife, which He Himself would do to wayward Israel if they would repent of their former ways. He would gladly accept them back from their exile. This resulted in the repentance He so patiently awaited. This paved the way for a whole nation to return to God.

> And the number of the sons of Israel will be like the sand on the seashore, which cannot be measured or counted. In the place where they were told, "You are no people of mine," they will be called, "The sons of the living God." The sons of Judah and Israel will be one again and choose themselves one single leader, and they will spread far beyond their country; so great will be the day of Jezreel. To your brother say, "People-of-Mine," to your sister, "Beloved."[30]

> But you must return to your God; maintain love and justice, and wait for your God always (Hosea 12:6 NIV).

We don't hear of Gomer cheating again. Maybe she liked this more authoritative approach, or maybe she realized, like Israel, that without a husband she can love and who truly loves her, life is futile. Spending a lifetime with someone who doesn't count your faults and failures is the best thing that could ever happen to her or any of us.

This is true love.

> Love suffers long and is kind; love does not envy; love does not parade itself; is not puffed up; does not behave

---

29. Footnote from Hosea 3:1, *New King James Version: Life Application Study Bible* (United States: Tyndale House Publishers, Incorporated, 1996), 1527.

30. Footnote from Hosea 3—The Great Future, *The Jerusalem Bible, Reader's Edition*, (Garden City, NY: Double Day and Company Inc., 1968), 1260.

rudely, does not seek its own, is not provoked, thinks no
evil; does not rejoice in iniquity, but rejoices in the truth;
bares all things, believes all things, hopes all things,
endures all things (1 Corinthians 13:4-7).

Imagine being with a Husband who proudly claims you for
Himself?

For I am jealous over you, with Godly jealousy: for I
have prepared you for one husband, to present you as a
pure virgin to Christ (2 Corinthians 11:2).

Quickly, I want to address all widows, widowers, single parents, and
unmarried adults. Where does this leave you? If you are in Christ, you
already have a Husband. Paul suggested if you can handle going without
the distraction of a husband or wife that would be even better.

But I want you to be without care. He who is unmarried
cares for the things of the Lord-how he may please the
Lord. And this I say for your own profit, not that I may put
a leash on you, but for what is proper, and that you may
serve the Lord without distraction (1 Corinthians 7:32,35).

There is no greater feeling than knowing you are in right standing
with God.

Let's momentarily look at what separated God from His chosen people. Knowing that these two stories intentionally mirror one another, be
mindful of any similar sins in your life that need to be addressed and
removed through repentance. Or, as you will see at first, there may not
be blatant sin but there are "controversies" that separate you and God,
disallowing fellowship and intimacy. If you say you can't hear God,
maybe it's due to a lack of knowledge resulting in a lack of faith.

> Hear the word of the Lord, ye children of Israel: for the Lord hath a controversy with the inhabitants of the land, because there is no truth, nor mercy, nor knowledge of God in the land (Hosea 4:1).

This is easily remedied if your heart is right.

> Faith comes by hearing and hearing by the Word of God (Romans 10:17).

In other words read, read, read the Bible, especially in these controversial days. Verse 2 speaks of commandments that are ignored. I know many who claim to be Christians but will take the Lord's name in vain with no second thought. They say that's not what they meant. Well, what did they mean?

> By swearing and lying, and killing, and stealing, and committing adultery, they break out, and blood toucheth blood (Hosea 4:2).

These and more sins such as idolatry are included, leading to the judgment of God's withdrawal.

> They go with their flocks and with their herds to seek the Lord; but they shall not find him, he hath withdrawn himself from them (Hosea 5:6).

That is probably the worst thing that can happen to an individual or a nation short of going to hell for all eternity. According to *Merriam-Webster's Collegiate Dictionary, idolatry* means "devotion to something." Ouch! If that didn't hurt, what does? Maybe it's time for some introspection. I hear you and I'm right there with you.

In the end, Hosea got what God knew to be the desire of his heart—a grateful wife along with a loving and devoted family complete in Him.

And delight thyself in the Lord, and he shall give thee thine heart's desire (Psalms 37:4).

Israel and Judah were forgiven and once again restored to Him.

I will heal their disloyalty, I will love them with all my heart, for my anger has turned from them. I will fall like dew on Israel. He shall bloom like the lily, and thrust out roots like the poplar, his shoots will spread far; he will have the beauty of the olive and the fragrance of Lebanon (Hosea 14:4-6).

These precious words are not limited to Israel and Judah; they are for us as well. Hallelujah! I know this as sure as I know my own name. Read on:

Now thanks be to God who always leads us in triumph in Christ, and through us diffuses the fragrance of His knowledge in every place. For we are to God the fragrance of Christ among those who are being saved and among those who are perishing. To the one we are the aroma of death, leading to death, and to the other we are the aroma of life leading to life (2 Corinthians 2:14-16a).

Which way will you lead them?

Chapter Six

Loving the Unlovely: King Manasseh

This story is for those men and women who literally hate themselves, i.e., hate what they've become; hate who they are or what they represent; hate that they've wasted their lives or spent their lives pursuing the wrong goals, believing the wrong things; hate how they have hurt so many others; hate that their life is one big zero. Yet by the tender mercy of God, one small touch from Him can turn your life around in a moment. With His love and forgiveness, you can dare to feel loved again. Let God respond to your penitence fully. Allow His forgiveness to saturate you. Experience the cleansing so thoroughly that it opens your heart to forgive others and even yourself. "It's up to us to allow God to draw us in. It's up to us to allow Him to love us the way He wants to love us. Allow God's intimacy to come and invade your heart. Ask Him what do you have in store for US today?"[31]

Cruelty can be turned around in a heartbeat. God's expansive love covers a multitude of sins. His blessings usually extend beyond the one and cover untold numbers of people and generations. Here is a case

31. James Rhine FB live, "Words of Encouragement," 6.23.2021.

where God does just that for a king's sake, a nation's sake, and all of their physical and spiritual seeds.

King Manasseh is the perfect case study—a smart man who did everything despicably wrong. Something drove him to undo in his miserable life all the good his father had accomplished until it was too late, but not too late for God with whom all things are possible. The 14th king of Judah, Manasseh was born into royalty. He was the only son of King Hezekiah, who was celebrated as one of the greatest kings Judah (the southern kingdom) ever had. Hezekiah reigned 29 years (715 B.C.). He destroyed all the images, groves, high places, and altars in Judah, Benjamin, Ephraim, and Manasseh. Because of King Hezekiah, all idolatry ended. He organized order among the priests and Levites. Each family, including wives, sons, and daughters, had their duties and orders by rotation all throughout Judah. He did right before the Lord. He restored and purified the Temple. He reopened the doors and reinstituted worship and oblations (orchestra, incense, and sacrifice) once again.

> And in every work that he began in the service of the house of God, and in the law, and in the commandments, to seek his God, he did it with all his heart, and prospered (2 Chronicles 31:21).

Realizing Jerusalem would be under attack after Judah was sieged and that Assyria was closing in, King Hezekiah encouraged the people to stand strong and firm in the face of the blaspheming king of Assyria, Sennacherib. In preparation for the inevitable affront, Hezekiah cut off the water supply from the out-skirting brook, then fortified the city by repairing the walls, adding towers and building a second wall. In addition, he made large numbers of missiles and shields. He was a good tactician and strategist. Despite the incredible opposition, he remained a man full of faith. Together with the great prophet Isaiah, Hezekiah prayed and cried to heaven. And in response, heaven heard and destroyed Sennacherib's army.

And the Lord sent an angel, which cut off all the mighty men of valour, and the leaders and captains in the camp of the king of Assyria. So he returned with shame of face to his own land. And when he was come into the house of his god, they that came forth of his own bowels slew him there with the sword. Thus the Lord saved Hezekiah and the inhabitants of Jerusalem from the hand of Sennacherib the king of Assyria, and from the hand of all others, and guided them on every side. And many brought gifts unto the Lord to Jerusalem, and brought presents to Hezekiah king of Judah; so that he was magnified in the sight of all nations from thenceforth (2 Chronicles 32:21-23).

Even though the Assyrians were temporarily defeated, they kept their eyes on the weak and vulnerable remainder of Israel. Aggressive and ambitious nations will wait like a big wild cat for the precise moment to pounce. That is why we must be vigilant to pray for America all of the time. What you see in the news is pitifully small compared to the huge plan that Satan has to rob, kill, and destroy us. You don't have to choose sides, but you do need to pray. Investors do this all the time. When the market and investments take a downturn, they pounce. When the value of a property goes down or even gold, silver, or precious metals, a good investor will rake it up at a convenient price and wait it out. The market will eventually turn around and the opportunity will be ripe to sell or strike.

Hezekiah, a type of Christ, had great influence over his people. When he became proud, the people became proud, which cost them dearly. When he humbled himself, the people also became humble. This kind of magnetism can prove detrimental if you're a leader and you're not walking closely with the Lord. Hezekiah became super rich. God gave him immense possessions, but judgment was coming because of a mistake he made when walking in pride.

Hezekiah was succeeded by Manasseh, merely a boy. Not enough evil things can be said about this young person. Where Hezekiah was day, Manasseh was night. Oddly, Manasseh was the longest reigning king in all of Israel. He served 55 years and devastated Judah for 16 of them. It's as though through his reign Israel had slipped into the "twilight zone." He did not have one redeeming quality. He was completely and totally morally corrupt. So how could things have gone so terribly wrong?

Manasseh means "one who causes to forget; forgetting; forgetfulness; causing forgetfulness; to be forgotten." Does this mean Manasseh came and went because his life was so insignificant that people don't remember him? Have you ever heard of King Manasseh, his great feats, or his failures? Or, could it mean Manasseh himself caused his people to forget God and everything they were taught to believe? If this is the case, Manasseh has a heavy burden to bear. Let's find out which definition applies.

Manasseh was 12 years old when he began to reign. His father, King Hezekiah, had just died at the age of 54. Let's stop a moment. Think—where was your head at the age of twelve? You would be at the top of middle school. Who were your biggest influences—your parents, immediate family, extended family, friends, teachers? This is hard to imagine, but if I were in charge of the southern part of my own country, my biggest influences would have been my parents and the government preceding me. In Manasseh's case, he had both. Yet it seemed he was under some kind of control outside of all of these things. He instituted laws and made changes in religious practices that were quite contrary to the godly precepts that Hezekiah had reinstated going back to King David's superior reign.

Satan was so enraged with the great moral reforms Hezekiah had achieved, he sought to undo all of his good works; hence the idea of creating Hezekiah's antithesis from his own loins. He used a young, impressionable, and foolish boy/man who had the means and authority to effectuate the fantastic and bazaar in order to shock the nation into submission. Manasseh was lured by former kings, dispossessed heathen, and exiled Jews into imitating their ungodly behavior. He brought what was left of Israel to its knees—Satan's dream.

> But he [King Ahaz] walked in the way of the kings of Israel; indeed he made his sons pass through the fire, according to the abomination of the nations whom the Lord had cast out before the children of Israel. And he sacrificed and burned incense on the high places, on the hills, and under every green tree (2 Kings 16:3-4).

> And he [Manasseh] did evil in the sight of the Lord, according to the abominations of the nations whom the Lord had cast out before the children of Israel. For he rebuilt the high places which Hezekiah his father had destroyed; he raised up altars for Baal, and made a wooden image, as Ahab king of Israel had done; and he worshiped all the host of heaven and served them (2 Kings 21:2-3).

In 697, Manasseh took the helm for 16 uninterrupted years. The northern kingdom had collapsed 25 years earlier with much of the population taken to Assyria under King Shalmaneser. This marked the end of the kings of Israel. The kings of Judah, in the southern region, would stay intact another 136 years before being carried away to Babylon by King Nebuchadnezzar. Between the ages of 12 and 25 Manasseh enforced horrific changes. Manasseh served in the highest position of public office. His transgressions are chronicled or referenced in many sources including three books of the Bible. Therefore, I will attempt to list the worst of his exceedingly contemptuous transgressions.

Even though one sin will separate us from God, Manasseh's were exacerbated by multiple violations of the laws and commandments of the God of Israel. God Himself expressly chose Israel to reveal Himself to the entire world. He promised to put His name in Jerusalem and be a "presence" there forever if His commandments were obeyed. The Lord even spoke to Manasseh and to his people, and tried to warn him through the prophets but HE was ignored (2 Chron. 33:10)

Manasseh erected pagan altars in the temple, enough for all of the host of heaven—sun, moon, and stars—and paid homage to these celestial bodies and promoted astral cults throughout his kingdom. He filled the courts of the temple with ungodly heathen altars for the common people to replicate. He then did the unthinkable. He sacrificed his own child (many sources say children) to Molech, the chief deity of the Ammonites, just as King Ahaz of Judah, Manasseh's paternal grandfather, had done a little over 35 years prior. He instituted witchcraft, soothsaying (fortune telling) and sorcery, consorted with wizards, necromancers (those who try to conjure up the dead), and yoked with a familiar spirit everywhere within his domain. "He did much evil in the sight of the Lord, to provoke Him to anger" (2 Kings 21:6). These acts are strictly forbidden by God because they demonstrate a lack of faith in Him, involve sinful actions, and open the door to demonic influences. They are counterfeits of God's power and have at their root a system of beliefs totally opposed to God.[32]

He led all of Judah down the primrose path of destruction. He had the people take part in every wrong or destructive act you can imagine. Manasseh misled Judah and the inhabitants of Jerusalem to commit more evil than all the dispossessed heathen before him. He reinstituted polytheistic worship. If the people couldn't be seduced into participating in these *abominations*—taken from the Hebrew word *toebah,* "anything that disgusts Almighty God, something that makes Him sick"—they were murdered or sacrificed. He committed ample evil to vex God. He purposefully provoked Him to anger.

---

32. Footnote from 2 Kings 21:6, *New King James Version: Life Application Study Bible* (United States: Tyndale House Publishers, Incorporated, 1996), 658.

And he caused his children to pass through the fire in the Valley of the Son of Hinnom: also he observed the times, and used enchantments, and used witchcraft, and dealt with a familiar spirit, and with wizards; he wrought much evil in the sight of the Lord, to provoke him to anger (2 Chronicles 33:6).

Rebellion of this magnitude, especially at such a young age, indicates something very dark and sinister, but what could it be? If it were possible, King Hezekiah would have been rolling over in his grave for such treason. Manasseh rebuilt all the shrines that his father had torn down. He built altars for Baal. *Baal* is "a Phoenician (Canaanite) deity originating along the coast of the Mediterranean Sea often used with another noun to lend specificity; a mastery of; to have dominion over; to be a husband of." This fake entity gave people a false sense of security and approval. Manasseh carved an image of *Asherah*—"star; a Canaanite goddess, a mistress of Baal," which escalated to temple prostitution. He set this image up in the temple just as King Ahab of Israel had done 156 years earlier. Prior to Manasseh, Ahab was considered the most evil king over all of Israel: *"For there was no one who sold himself to do evil in the sight of the Lord as did Ahab, incited by his wife Jezebel"* (1 Kings 21:25). Now Manasseh was considered the most evil king over all of Judah.

When Manasseh desecrated the temple in this manner, he became a type of antichrist. He murdered, he plundered, he profaned God's temple. His sacrilegious acts prepared the way for the most wicked man yet to walk the face of the earth—the Antichrist. During the last half of the tribulation, toward the end of his torturous reign, he will set up the "abomination of desolation" in the temple when everyone is advised to run for the hills and caves. He will bring about the end of the world as we know it by way of the tribulation. The spirit of *antichrist,* which means "adversary to Christ, against Christ, an opponent of Messiah," exists today and has since Satan arrived as a roaring lion to seek whom he may devour (1 Peter 5:8). This spirit opposes Christ and will undermine Him at every opportunity.

> Now brother will betray brother to death, and a father his child; and children will rise up against parents and cause them to be put to death. And you will be hated for My name's sake. But he who endures to the end will be saved. So when you see the 'abomination of desolation,' spoken of by Daniel the prophet, standing where it ought not then let those who are in Judea flee to the mountains (Mark 13:12-14).

> And every spirit that confesseth not that Jesus Christ is come in the flesh is not of God: and this is that spirit of antichrist, whereof ye have heard that it should come; and even now already is it in the world (1 John 4:3).

Manasseh worshiped his own god. Which god was that? He seemed to be taken by all of them. I've known people who prayed to everything in order to "be covered." I once worked for a brilliant doctor from Taiwan. She claimed to be a Buddhist but acknowledged many gods. She sternly told me not to talk about my God because, sadly, she thought she was better off praying to the many. Make no mistake, God is a jealous God and will have no other gods before Him. On the contrary, Satan is the god behind every masked entity using the guise of something or someone else. He is our true enemy, yet he can't hold a stick to us if we believe in the one true God.

> Little children, ye are of God, and have overcome them: for greater is he that is in you, than he that is in the world (1 John 4:4).

Satan is the evil spirit associated with all the Baals, Asherahs, carved images of gold and wood, Molech, all the philosophies and religions

108

that exclude Jesus Christ as the second person of the triune Godhead—the Son of God. Satan is the one false god behind every lifeless god that exists. If you don't belong to God Almighty, you belong to him. Plain and simple.

Manasseh had literally gone off his rocker. He certainly committed enough atrocities for Satan to gain possession. It would take God—the true God of the universe, the God of Abraham, Isaac, and Jacob, Elohim, Father, Son, and Holy Spirit—to pull him out of this one. Manasseh not only defiled the temple but barbarously slew all the righteous men, even the prophets.[33] Many sources believe that Manasseh was responsible for the annihilation of one of the greatest prophets who ever lived. *Isaiah,* which means "the Lord is salvation," died just before Manasseh was captured. Because scripture alludes to Isaiah being sawn in half and because it was common practice for Manasseh to kill the prophets, it is believed Manasseh himself ordered the hideous execution of this spiritually prolific man.

> Manasseh also sacrificed many innocent people, till he filled Jerusalem with murders from end to end, besides the sin into which he led Judah by doing evil in the sight of the Eternal (2 Kings 21:16).

> They were stoned, they were sawn in two, were tempted, were slain with the sword. They wandered about in sheepskins and goatskins, being destitute, afflicted, tormented- of whom the world was not worthy (Hebrews 11:37-38a).

Isaiah was a major classical and literary prophet who wrote prophetic works during the lifetime of Hezekiah and Manasseh. He was Manasseh's maternal grandfather. He consulted directly with King Hezekiah on a number of important issues, including Hezekiah's

---

33. *JOSEPHUS: Complete Works.* (Grand Rapids, MI: Kregel Publications, 1981), 214.

merciful healing extending his life 15 more years (Isa. 38:5) and the imminent consequence of judgment and captivity as a result of his unfounded pride. In the book named after himself, Isaiah prophesied the virgin birth and the crucifixion of Messiah (Isa. 7:14; 53:7-8). He prophesied the destruction (primarily due to idolatry) and the restoration of Jerusalem and Judah. He warned how Assyria would be the oppressive destroyer that would punish the disobedient Jews leaving only a remnant culminating in Assyria's own destruction because of their excessive cruelty and insolence (Isa. 27:7-13; 30:31). He made proclamations against many countries, including Babylon (Isa. 21:9). He faithfully praised God and composed a song of salvation for Judah, which ironically included the line, "Let grace be shown to the wicked" (Isa. 26:10). Here, he may have been interceding for his own executioner. He spoke of the fall of Lucifer (renamed Satan by God Himself) and his ultimate destruction due to pride (Isa. 14:12-19). He spoke of the remission of sins and exhorted all to come to his "Servant the Savior" (Isa. 53:5-12; 45:22). He presented Jesus as the "Hope of Salvation" to the tribes of Israel and as a "Light" to the Gentiles (Isa. 49:5-6).

The *Pseudepigrapha* includes a non-canonical book known as "The Ascension of Isaiah," which is divided into three main sections. The first refers to the martyrdom of Isaiah himself. While historians believe this writing to be fiction, ancient Jewish tradition suggests that Isaiah was martyred by Manasseh. It is described in the book that Isaiah was tied inside a sack, placed within the hollow of a tree trunk, then sawed in two with a wooden saw. Additionally, the Talmud (a collection of Jewish texts that record the oral tradition of the early rabbis) records Isaiah hid inside a cedar tree and when discovered was executed in the same manner.[34]

God said, *"Enough!"* God sent Assyrian generals and captains in 680 B.C. They caught, chained, and shackled Manasseh and put hooks

---

34. "How did Isaiah Die?," Got Questions Ministries, accessed July 8, 2022, https://www.gotquestions.org/how-did-Isaiah-die.html.

in his nose and carried him off to Babylon, then a vassal state. There is not much explanation proffered as to why the Assyrians dragged Manasseh to Babylon rather than to Assyria. Between 652 and 646 B.C., the city of Babylon rebelled against Assyria. The rebellion was crushed, but Assyria may have suspected that Manasseh supported it. That may explain why Manasseh was taken to Babylon for trial rather than to the Assyrian capital of Nineveh.[35]

> Therefore, the Lord brought upon them the captains of the army of the King of Assyria, who took Manasseh with hooks, bound him with bronze fetter's and carried him off to Babylon (2 Chronicles 33:11).

Hooked to a wall by his fettered feet behind him while on his knees on a cold, hard, filthy floor holding a plank on his shoulders with holes to put his arms through, leaning forward with head forced into a bowed position, Manasseh woke up from the nightmare he had been living and causing. He knew he was the cause of all the misery and the decrepit condition he had led the nation into and that it was wrong in the sight of Almighty God.

God was so enraged with His people and the false prophets that, in addition to the famine, He promised four kinds of death, all because of what Manasseh did.

> Then the Lord said to me (Jeremiah), "Even if Moses and Samuel stood before Me, My mind would not be favorable toward this people. Cast them out of my sight, and let them go forth. 'And I will appoint over them four forms of destruction," says the Lord: "the sword to slay, the dogs to drag, the birds of the heavens and the beasts of the earth to devour and destroy. I will hand them

---

35. Footnote from 2 Chronicles 33:11, *New King James Version: Life Application Study Bible* (United States: Tyndale House Publishers, Incorporated, 1996), 768.

over to trouble, to all kingdoms of the earth, because of Manasseh the son of Hezekiah, king of Judah, for what he did in Jerusalem. "For who will have pity on you, O Jerusalem? Or who will bemoan you? Or who will turn aside to ask how you are doing? You have forsaken Me," says the Lord, "You have gone backward. Therefore, I will stretch out My hand against you and destroy you; I am weary of relenting! (Jeremiah 15:1-6)

Manasseh, sitting in his cell, was forced to realize that Israel was now paying the price for his sin. However, through his confinement he found humility. It would seem the satanic veil lifted long enough for him to fully appreciate his distressful and painful reality both physically and spiritually. It was here that Manasseh finally came to the end of himself. Let us hope you will not have to reach a similar rock bottom or be fettered to a wall in order to come to your senses. Simply put, Manasseh begged God for forgiveness. Now here comes the amazing part. God not only heard him, he answered him. Then and only then he knew God was real and could forgive him.

Now when he was in affliction, he implored the Lord his God, and humbled himself greatly before the God of his fathers and prayed to Him; and He received his entreaty, heard his supplication, and brought him back to Jerusalem into his kingdom. Then Manasseh knew that the Lord was God (2 Chronicles 33:12-13).

If you can relate to years of unadulterated sin in which your heart becomes so hard, it becomes very difficult to imagine yourself worthy of anything good and decent. Your hope is gone. You were a mistake. It would have been better if you were never born, or so you might think. Aren't you relieved to learn God's thoughts are much higher than our thoughts? We keep forgetting that God allowed us in this world already knowing every sin we would ever commit. It's you He loves! He had a plan to bring you back to Himself even before you were born. To make it easy for you, it's not that God can't forgive you; it's you thinking you are not worthy of His forgiveness. That's correct. You are not. None of us are. That's why, through Christ, we are made worthy. If we take on His sacrifice by making Him our personal Savior, then, essentially, He becomes our substitute by suffering and dying for us. He didn't ask us. He just did it because He loves us. Please don't waste His sacrifice on a lifelong pity party. Get smart like Manasseh, who learned from his mistakes. Give it over to God, who nailed your sins to the very cross on which He hung for you and for me.

The Sins of Our Fathers

Allow me to insert a deep and personal testimony that I think fits into this story. Both my father and paternal grandfather were boxers in the navy. They were very strict, short-tempered, and extremely conservative. My grandfather was devoted to my granny. As far back as I remember, he was already walking with the Lord. Rarely did I see him without a Bible in his hand. He seemed very sweet and endearing. He always wanted to be with family and spend time teaching me new things biblically related. According to my mother, he wasn't always that way. Since I have no proof, I will not dwell on the things she shared. However, if he did treat Dad with rough physical correction while growing up, he certainly was a changed man when he found the Lord, or it could've been that Dad just needed to grow up. Either way, I loved Pop Pop very much.

Dad, on the other hand, had to be in control, and he was prone to alcohol consumption. If you went against him, no matter who you were, he would get physical. Even during tickle time he was so rough that I couldn't breathe. His physical confrontations with the other men in town made him very unpopular. It seemed every week he would take some guy outside the bar and throw the deciding punch before the poor guy even got out a word. He knocked them out with a single blow.

113

When I was ten years old it was a big deal for all the kids to jump off the Vincentown dam. It was plenty deep and seemed perfectly safe. My dad warned me not to do it. He didn't care if all the other kids did it. He said *no!* Well you know I had to do it—everybody else did and I wanted to be cool like them. The second to last time I jumped I got caught red handed. He took me home and, while still in my wet bathing suit, beat me with a leather belt until it literally broke in half. The welts lasted for weeks. My mother was too scared to do anything. Occasionally she took a swipe that was meant for me. Yet she constantly reminded me that "Your father does love you." His favorite form of punishment was to kick me against the wall then put me on a harsh restriction for months at a time.

As an only child living in the pine barrens, life seemed unbearable at times. Lots of kids, including my own cousins, were jealous of me. They didn't know what happened behind closed doors. All they saw were my minibike, rabbits, pony, and a handful of horses. We lived on a small ranch. One by one I lost them all because Dad got mad about something so much smaller by contrast. He even made me tell potential buyers how great the horses were so they would want to buy them. To this day I find myself forgiving Dad at least once a week. I really mean it each time, but old wounds keep resurfacing. And yes, I jumped off the dam one more time after that. It was exhilarating!

At the age of 45, Dad moved to West Virginia almost 500 miles away and started a whole new life. My mother left him one year earlier telling me I was an adult now, at 18 her duty to me was over. I could go with her if I chose. She would not stay with him one more day. Dad remarried about three years later and I could see the same pattern starting all over again with his new wife. At times he would be endearing, other times he would be mocking and mean toward her. Twelve years later I got saved. I gave my life to Jesus and couldn't wait to tell Dad. He called me a hypocrite. I was not sure why he thought that, probably because I had become very rebellious. My rebellious act started when I was 13 or 14. I even remember telling God one morning that I was taking a break from Him. One day I would return to Him. Can you imagine? Thank God for His mercy and that He allowed me to live long enough, almost 17 years later, to do just that. Yet, it took a lifetime to prove to Dad my life really belonged to Jesus.

He didn't have much faith in my academic prowess either. He believed women shouldn't bother with college. They ought to be hair dressers or secretaries only. As noble as these professions are, neither interested me. I enrolled in a teacher's college and graduated with a BA and an M.Ed. and earned five certifications. Each time, I sent him the formal documents to try to make him proud of me.

Finally, one day while visiting him, at the dinner table he said out of the blue, "I could have gone to jail for what I done to you." I didn't know what to say so I said nothing. Another time he told me, "God could never forgive me for what I done." He said it the same weird way. I assured him God could and wanted to forgive him. All he had to do was ask. Eventually, I told him I forgave him too. It took 35 years of witnessing to him to finally convince him. He knew if God could make me into the woman I became, leaving all that rebellion behind, He could do anything, even forgive him.

Dad died at the ripe old age of 94 as a believing, born again son of the loving, forgiving Lord God. His last words to me while holding both of my hands in what were once iron fists were, "I love you, babe, and I'm proud of you. You don't have to worry about me because I love God with all my heart and I know He loves me."

Like my father, Manasseh seemed unlovable. You may ask, "How could God possibly forgive Manasseh?" It seems like God went way out of His way to bring Manasseh to that broken state in order to give him an opportunity to repent. However, forgiveness is limited not by the amount of sin but by our willingness to repent.[36]

What about those who never heard of Jesus? What about the guy who lives alone on an island? Well, God has a way of reaching everyone. Those

---

36. Insert about Manasseh, *New King James Version: Life Application Study Bible* (United States: Tyndale House Publishers, Incorporated, 1996), 769.

of you who have read this book can see and share what great things God will do for those who cry out to Him; call on His name, believe by faith, and trust in Him. Romans 1 says that everyone will know He exists by what they see in nature.

God has a way of speaking to the heart, even through creation. As an example, I've actually met the illusion guy who lives alone on an island when I went to Brazil. I went on an evening excursion along the Amazon River with a Chinese girl, the native guide, and the captain of the boat. It was very different from anything I had ever done. We went slowly down the river with only the moon and a lantern to guide us. We finally got to our destination, a tiny island, and landed for the evening. A man who looked to be 50 came running out to greet us. He had a hut further in the woods and stayed with us while we went swimming and ate fresh fish by the fire. My new friend and I wanted to go back in the river, but the guide emphatically told us no. Upon further inquiry, he explained that piranha were all around, and we would be risking it were we to go in again. We were shocked that he let us go in the first place, but at least we now understood why he kept making so much noise and roughing up the water the first time. We went back to our boat for the night before going back the next morning. While I didn't try to talk to the guy on the island about Jesus (as he did not speak English), I did pray with my two young comrades on the way there to receive Christ. Maybe God will use the guide or someone else who visits that area to tell the island guy. In the course of a week, I would estimate he meets a dozen people who come from all over the world for that kind of adventure. Turns out he wasn't so alone after all!

Once Manasseh was released, he made changes under his new leadership. While in Babylon, Manasseh was molded into proper vassal behavior and Israel became a vassal state. A vassal person, state, or country is subservient to another more powerful entity in exchange for some kind of service or money. It would be 56 years before Babylon overthrew Assyria, making them the leading ruler of the Middle East. Meanwhile, Israel was subject to Assyria's leadership who now became the feudal country or overseer. In return for homage and monetary tribute, they provided Israel with protection and allegiance.

Manasseh served under King Esarhaddon until his death in 668 B.C., then served under King Assurbanipal for the remainder of his 55 years as king. Manasseh did productive things for the rural economy and sought to reverse every sacrilegious infraction he imposed upon his people (2 Chron. 33:14-16). Upon his return to Jerusalem, he endeavored to forget his former sins against God, of which he now repented, and applied himself to a very religious life. Manasseh was solely intent on returning his sincere thanks to God for his deliverance and preserving a lifelong relationship of gratitude and servitude.[37]

Manasseh's reforms were twofold—spiritualistic and militaristic. He immediately sanctified the temple and purged the city of all witchcraft, occult images, and forbidden places of worship. He instructed the people to avoid all temptation to partake in these vile practices. He rebuilt the altar and offered the appropriate sacrifices with the appropriate curators to administer them. In an effort to further secure Jerusalem, he also fortified (doubled) and rebuilt the walls, then he strengthened the garrisons with manpower and provisions. He became a role model for his people to imitate while the healing spread throughout the land. He was deemed a happy man both from the time of his redemption by God and restoration to the throne.

The Prayer of Manasseh is referenced in 2 Chronicles 33:13, 18-19, so I thought it was worth mentioning here. Clearly it is a prayer that Ezra, the author of 1 and 2 Chronicles, and the Seers or early Jewish writers wanted recorded. To me, it is Manasseh's personal prayer of contrition except that it was written approximately 108 B.C. by an anonymous author. It is a replica of what the author believed Manasseh would have said. This particular prayer was included in many sources and early Bibles including the original 1611 King James Version. It is now considered apocryphal or non-canonical due to its non-authenticity.

37.*JOSEPHUS: Complete Works.* (Grand Rapids, MI: Kregel Publications, 1981), 215. https://quod.lib.umich.edu/cgi/k/kjv/kjv-idx?type=DIV1&byte=4140878.

Lord, Almighty God of our fathers, Abraham, Isaac, and Jacob, and of their righteous seed; who hast made heaven and earth, with all the ornament thereof; who hast bound the sea by the word of thy commandment; who hast shut up the deep, and sealed it by thy terrible and glorious name; whom all men fear, and tremble before thy power; for the majesty of thy glory cannot be borne, and thine angry threatening toward sinners is importable: but thy merciful promise is unmeasurable and unsearchable; for thou art the most high Lord, of great compassion, longsuffering, very merciful, and repentest of the evils of men. Thou, O Lord, according to thy great goodness hast promised repentance and forgiveness to them that have sinned against thee: and of thine infinite mercies hast appointed repentance unto sinners, that they may be saved. Thou therefore, O Lord, that art the God of the just, hast not appointed repentance to the just, as to Abraham, and Isaac, and Jacob, which have not sinned against thee; but thou hast appointed repentance unto me that am a sinner: for I have sinned above the number of the sands of the sea. My transgressions, O Lord, are multiplied: my transgressions are multiplied, and I am not worthy to behold and see the height of heaven for the multitude of mine iniquities. I am bowed down with many iron bands, that I cannot lift up mine head, neither have any release: for I have provoked thy wrath, and done evil before thee: I did not thy will, neither kept I thy commandments: I have set up abominations, and have multiplied offenses. Now therefore I bow the knee of mine heart, beseeching thee of grace. I have sinned, O Lord, I have sinned, and I acknowledge mine iniquities: wherefore, I humbly beseech thee, forgive me, O Lord, forgive me, and destroy me not with mine iniquities. Be not angry with me for ever, by reserving evil for me; neither condemn me to the lower parts of the earth. For thou art the God, even the God of them that repent; and in

me thou wilt shew all thy goodness: for thou wilt save me,
that am unworthy, according to thy great mercy. Therefore
I will praise thee for ever all the days of my life: for all the
powers of the heavens do praise thee, and thine is the glory
for ever and ever. Amen.

With every action there is a reaction. Sin will be forgiven, which is
the point of this entire chapter no matter who you are. Whether you are a
reprisal of my Dad or Manasseh, with confession comes God's mercy, compassion, and forgiveness. However, the consequence of sin is a whole other
matter. Let's take Manasseh's son *Amon* for instance. Next to leading the
southern half of Israel astray, I believe Amon's short story is one of the sad-
dest of all. He rebelled against God, following his father's early example.
Unlike Manasseh, Amon didn't get the time to rethink his actions, examine
his heart toward the God of his fathers, and make the turn around that his
father did.

The type of mistakes Amon committed were spiritual because they
involved Israel turning away from God. As Manasseh sacrificed his son(s),
he also sacrificed Amon, his successor to the throne. He knew how much he
was devoted to him. Amon's name means *faithful*. At the age of 22 Amon
followed in his father's original footsteps. His every step caused his heart
to get harder and harder. In the end, after only two years on the throne,
Amon was killed by his own servants in his own house—lost, never to be
retrieved. Decisions you make today will have lasting consequences for you
and those around you. Remember that.

Hopefully you have come clean with God. Every day I ask Him to forgive me for the sins I've committed. Compared to what my sins were before
coming to Him, they are extremely small, yet a sin is a sin and each has a
consequence—anywhere from guilt leading to condemnation or to some
great loss, like ruining my witness to talk about Jesus. Manasseh repented
of his ways yet could not bring his children back to the Lord. When King
David sent the great and loyal soldier Uriah to the front lines all alone to
die, he repented but could not cleanse himself of his sexual sins and the

consequence of Bathsheba having his child. King Hezekiah repented for showing the Babylonian messengers all of his treasures but could not stop the onslaught of King Nebuchadnezzar to raid Jerusalem in order to enrich his country. You get the point.

Let's return to Manasseh. The Israelites did not support the murder of Amon so they installed his son, king Manasseh's grandson Josiah, in his place. Next to King David himself, Josiah is considered the best king Israel ever had. He did everything right in the eyes of God from his heart. He served God for 31 years and led the nation into one of their most glorious epochs. Everything was restored to God's standards and the people worshiped God and God only. This was also part of Manasseh's legacy.

Even though Manasseh restored Israel back to God, he has five rebukes as part of his legacy:

1) Two of the three books that mention his life (2 Kings and Jeremiah) don't include his repentance and restoration.

2) The one that does (2 Chronicles 33:18) ends Manasseh's story with the usual, "Now for the rest of the acts, his good deeds which are listed are written in the book of the kings of Israel." But then it goes on to say, "And all his sin and trespass, and the sites where he built high places and set up wooden images and carved images." More bad things are listed than good.

3) He was not buried in the tombs of his fathers but in the garden of his own house.

4) Less than one chapter is devoted to his reign despite the fact that he ruled for more than half a century.

5) His successes were expunged from the biblical record.[38]

38. "The Evil King Manasseh: Idolatry and Politics," Eli Kavon, *The Jerusalem Post*, published July 11, 2016, https://www.jpost.com/Opinion/The-evil-king-Manasseh-Idolatry-and-politics-460115.

We mustn't get upset with God for giving this personified devil, Manasseh, another chance. I believe he did it for us—for His people, then and now, down to the very last person, Jew and Gentile. He did it to reveal His true nature and to show us it's never too late as long as we draw breath. Unfortunately, we don't come with a timer—we don't know how many breaths we get. He has come so that none would perish, but come to know the truth. You reading this right here and right now is no coincidence. Two facts:

1) We are not promised tomorrow.

> The Lord is not slack concerning His promise, as some count slackness, but is longsuffering toward us, not willing that any should perish but that all should come to repentance (2 Peter 3:9).

> For He says: "In an acceptable time I have heard you, And in the day of salvation I have helped you." Behold, now is the accepted time; behold, now is the day of salvation (2 Corinthians 6:2).

2) God loves you no matter who you are or what you have done.

As with the prodigal son, He sees you from afar. He's coming toward you. Won't you take this opportunity to run into His arms? The sooner you embrace, the sooner your sins will be forgiven and forgotten.

> And he [prodigal son, second son] arose and came to his father, But when he was still a great way off, his father saw him and had compassion, and ran and fell on his neck and kissed him (Luke 15:20).

> As far as the east is from the west, So far has He removed our transgressions from us (Psalms 103:12).

121

Ask for forgiveness and move on with your life, a free person, a child of the great Deliverer, the Beginning and the End—the beginning of a new life in Christ and the end of a wasted life under Satan. Because of Jesus, you are worthy of forgiveness. Don't add rejection of Jesus and His cleansing blood to your list of regrets. He suffered excruciating pain and humiliation for *each and every one of us*. Make His death count for something by making your life count for something. By humbling yourself before God you are now finally in agreement with Him. He's been waiting for this moment. Talk to Him freely as you would to a friend. Humble yourself as did Jesus. Let the world see that you believed, then acted.

Manasseh repented and God gave him a second chance. God's reconciliation was real as He made way for him to be part of the Messiah's story. Saving the best for last, Manasseh's entire bloodline comprises the genealogy of Jesus Christ, dating back to Abraham and dating forward from Manasseh—father of Amon, father of Josiah, father of Jeconiah, the 70 years of exile, captivity, and release from Babylon notwithstanding, all the way to Jacob the father of Joseph, the husband of Mary, and the man who raised Jesus (Matt. 1:1-16). Despite the sins, frailties, and long sufferings these people had to endure and what they put God through with their failings, foolishness, and unfaithfulness, God remained faithful and true to His promise and covenant with Abraham. The stories we've read just prove that God takes ordinary and even bad people and turns them into extraordinary, devout people. This happens when we allow Him to mold and shape us into the people He desires, the purpose for which we were born.

Though Manasseh was once an evil man, a mass murderer, idol worshiper, and more, this story reveals God's vast and unlimited love for us. This story shows the love of God for even the least of these, even the unlovely.

Chapter Seven

Bond or Bondage: Daniel and Nebuchadnezzar

I s it possible to love a total stranger? How about one who is the leader of another country contrary to your entire way of life and belief system? Let me remind you of one of the Hebrew definitions of love, *ahab,* means "to love with an affection that carries an allegiance, dedication, and or loyalty." Furthermore, is it possible to have godly affection for someone who has taken you captive away from everything you hold dear to a country far away? Could you bring yourself to love, as defined in the Hebrew word *racham,* which means "have mercy, compassion, and even pity," for someone who ripped you from your home and took you 500 hundred miles away? You'd probably answer, *"Absolutely not!"* But if you allow God to direct you, He'll give you the peace to have *ahab* and *racham* for even the most bizarre captors.

How deep is our personal love and devotion to God in return for His redemption in Christ? Do we ever really reach the point where we say we've reached the mark? Probably not. Clearly a type of Christ, Daniel demonstrated purity in love and obedience. He was a focused individual, yet only a man. His trust in and love for God took him to levels most people never experience. He used his prowess and skill only for God's glory.

Eunuch

Eunuch in the Hebrew is *cariyc*; the Aramaic is *saris*. There are two distinct and separate definitions for the homonym *eunuch* prior to 1000 B.C. Since that time there are other words utilized that more clearly define the intended meaning. According to *The American Heritage Desk Dictionary*, there is only one definition for *eunuch,* which is "a castrated man, esp. one who was employed as a harem attendant." According to *Strong's Exhaustive Concordance of the Bible*, *eunuch* can also mean minister of the state, chamberlain, or officer. Why even insert this little anomaly? On top of everything else that happened to them, as you will soon read, what kind of men, what kind of character could Daniel have had that would bring him to forgive the one responsible for such a humiliating mutilation? Totally abhorred and rejected by his own country, he eventually won the prideful tyrant, Nebuchadnezzar, to glorify One greater than himself—the Lord God Almighty. Daniel, who loved God more than life itself, may have been the closest specimen to perfection who lived on this planet—aside from Jesus Christ, who never sinned once, not even from His heart. He may have been the only one who could change King Nebuchadnezzar's heart.

The Jews were marched under harsh conditions from Jerusalem north to Riblah (where they met up with King Nebuchadnezzar) along the Mediterranean Sea, continued north to Aleppo, then south to Babylon along the Euphrates River. Upon arrival, Daniel and his closest friends were immediately sent to the house of the eunuchs and mentored by the chief and his assistant. Then they were given special food to eat and assigned to learn the language, science, and customs of that foreign nation for the next three years in order to change their identities and prepare them for serving in the king's palace. For all they knew, their life as they once knew it was over. If you could eventually love the person responsible for doing something similar to you, then you and Daniel have something very special in common.

Let's begin at the beginning. Daniel was about 17 when he and his countrymen were captured. However, the book of Daniel was written by Daniel approximately 536 B.C., 69 years after he had been taken into captivity. This means he was close to 87 years old when he wrote the book. Most scholars agree that Daniel and his Hebrew companions, Hananiah, Mishael, and Azariah, were taken during the first wave under King Jehoiakim of Judah's reign. General Nebuzaradan, under Nebuchadnezzar's command, marched into Jerusalem and besieged the temple built by King Solomon over 470 years earlier. The temple was robbed of gold and silver vessels, its rulers, priests, royalty, and the very finest children of Israel. This capture of the Jewish people and Jerusalem was allowed by God.

> In the third year of the reign of Jehoiakim king of Judah, Nebuchadnezzar, king of Babylon, came to Jerusalem and besieged it. The Lord gave Jehoiakim king of Judah into his hand, with part of the vessels of the house of God, and he carried them into the land of Shinar to the house of his god (Daniel 1:1-2).

King Nebuchadnezzar, while still in his early twenties and very early in his career, was well on his way to establishing a reputation marked with violence and cruelty. Some of his favorite methods of annihilation were beheading, cremating while still alive, tearing limb from limb, or simply cutting people into little pieces. King Nebuchadnezzar administered the execution of King Zedekiah's sons, forcing him to watch then have his eyes gouged out. This would be the last thing he saw before being led in shackles to Babylon whereupon he, along with another leader, were burned to death in front of all the exiles.

Now Zedekiah rebelled against the king of Babylon. So in the ninth year of Zedekiah's reign, Nebuchadnezzar, king of Babylon marched against Jerusalem with his whole army. He encamped outside the city and built siege works all around it. The city was kept under siege until the eleventh year of King Zedekiah. The famine in the city had become so severe that there was no food for the people to eat. Then the city wall was broken through, and the whole army fled at night through the gate between the two walls near the king's garden, though the Babylonians were surrounding the city. They fled toward the Arabah, but the Babylonian army pursued the king and overtook him in the plains of Jericho. All his soldiers were separated from him and scattered, and he was captured. He was taken to the king of Babylon at Riblah, where sentence was pronounced on him. They killed the sons of Zedekiah before his eyes. Then they put out his eyes, bound him with bronze shackles and took him to Babylon (2 Kings 25:1-3,7).

Wow! Why? Why would God allow such a thing? In order that the prophecy of Isaiah 106 years earlier to King Hezekiah of Judah be fulfilled.

And Hezekiah hearkened unto them [Berodach-baladan, the son of Baladan, king of Babylon], and shewed them all the house of his precious things, the silver and the gold, and the spices, and the precious ointment, and all the house of his armour, and all that was found in his treasures: there was nothing in his house, nor in all his dominion, that Hezekiah shewed them not. Then came Isaiah the prophet unto king Hezekiah, and said unto him, What said these men? And from whence came they unto thee? And Hezekiah said, They are from a far country, even from Babylon.

And he said, What have they seen in thine house? And Hezekiah answered, All the things that are in mine house have they seen: There is nothing among my treasures that I have not shewed them. And Isaiah said unto Hezekiah, Hear the word of the Lord. Behold the days come, that all that is in thine house, and that which thy fathers have laid up in store unto this day, shall be carried into Babylon: nothing shall be left, saith the Lord. And of the sons that shall issue from thee, which thou shall beget, shall they take away; and they shall be eunuchs in the palace of the king of Babylon (2 Kings 20:13-18).

Daniel was considered a noble son of Israel with no blemish. In other words, he was handsome and skillful in every branch of learning and wisdom, gifted with understanding and discerning of knowledge. "Daniel is one of the few men of the Bible of whom only good things are recorded. He was a most commanding figure in intellectual ability, executive aptitude, personal virtue and infinite faith. He was chosen by the Babylonians as one of the most outstanding youth in Jerusalem."[39] He had the whole world ahead of him. *Daniel*, which means "God is my judge," was now renamed *Belteshazzer*, meaning "Bel or Baal protect the king." He began to win the hearts of the chief eunuch, Ashpenaz, the captain of the army or chief executioner, Arioch, and eventually the king himself even to the point where they all risked their reputation or life for him.

Now God had brought Daniel into favour and tender love
with the prince of the eunuchs (Daniel 1:9).

The word *love* used here is *egeb*, which means "much love, loving kindness, compassion, lovely."

39. Henry Feyerabend, *Daniel Verse by Verse*, (Oshawa, Ontario: Maracle Press Limited, 1990), 15.

In a very short amount of time Daniel won favor with Ashpenaz, who had love and compassion enough to risk endangering his head to the king. He permitted Daniel and his friends to stay on a strict diet of vegetables and legumes rather than eat the king's delicacies. As already noted, Daniel and his three companions had a special aptitude toward all literature and knowledge. In addition, Daniel was inspired in the area of visions and dreams. Nebuchadnezzar recognized their gifts, particularly Daniel's, in their very first meeting together. Being so highly skilled and intelligent immediately brought them into favor with Nebuchadnezzar.

In Nebuchadnezzar's second year, he had disturbing dreams "and his spirit was troubled." He demanded sorcerers, magicians, astrologers, and Chaldeans to tell him the dream as well as the interpretation. This order threatened merciless execution to all the "wise men" who served in the king's palace, including Daniel and his three companions. When Daniel, barely 20 years old, heard this he immediately sought Arioch. Imagine a 20-year-old, non-enlisted man demanding an audience with a 20-year career captain to question why the commander in chief was in such a hurry to eliminate the wise men.

> Therefore, Daniel went in unto Arioch, whom the king had ordained to destroy the wise men of Babylon. He went and said to him: "Do not destroy the wise men of Babylon. Bring me in before the king, and I will tell the king the interpretation" (Daniel 2:24).

"God brought about a love for Daniel in the heart of the court of the king."[40] Did he accomplish this because he served notably and respectfully while utilizing his gifts? Yes, but God had another purpose in mind as well. Daniel's righteous character did not require him to love with the *ahab*/affection or *racham*/compassion kind of love. But that eventually

---

40. Henry Feyerabend, *Daniel Verse by Verse*, (Oshawa, Ontario: Maracle Press Limited, 1990), 28.

softened his heart toward king Nebuchadnezzar." We will revisit this matter of the heart as we move forward.

Back to the dream—at first, I thought it was Nebuchadnezzar's arrogance that insisted all of his "wise men" tell him the dream to test their legitimacy. Upon closer look, I realized he actually forgot the dream.

> And the king said unto them [the wise men]. I have dreamed a dream, and my spirit was troubled to know the dream. Then spake the Chaldeans (Diviners) to the king in Syriack, O king, live for-ever: tell thy servants the dream, and we will shew the interpretation. The king answered and said to the Chaldeans, The thing is gone from me: if you will not make known unto me the dream, with the interpretation thereof, you shall be cut in pieces, and your houses shall be made a dunghill (Daniel 2:3-5).

The exchange between them was repeated, which served to activate the hideous death sentence. Arioch chose to delay the king's orders to slay the wise men in order to make the thing known to Daniel, which in and of itself was a great risk. Evidently, a kind of mutual respect must have existed between Arioch and Daniel. Not only did Arioch risk a severe rebuke by delaying the slaughter as Daniel requested, but he absolutely believed Daniel had the information Nebuchadnezzar wanted simply based on the word of a lad whom he trusted. Then Daniel went to the king himself to ask for a stay in their sentence in order to gain the time needed to get both the dream and its interpretation. "A king, and especially a king as powerful as Nebuchadnezzar, could not void a decree without proper cause."[41] While Daniel didn't actually say he and his companions would seek their God, I think this egomaniacal king knew that Daniel would fall on the mercy of God. Daniel knew

---

41. N.W. Hutchings, *Exploring the Book of Daniel*, (Oklahoma City, OK: Hearthstone Publishing, 1990), 36.

Nebuchadnezzar would kill him, he just didn't know if he would grant him the time.

> So Daniel went in and asked the king that he would give him time, that he might tell [the king] the interpretation. Then Daniel went to his house, and made the decision known to Hananiah, Mishael, Azariah, his companions, that they would desire mercies of the God of heaven concerning this secret; that Daniel and his fellows should not perish with the rest of the wise men of Babylon (Daniel 2:16-18).

God was gracious to His servant Daniel and revealed the king's dream and its meaning to him. Daniel's success in both relaying and interpreting Nebuchadnezzar's dream accomplished a lot of things: first, it relieved Nebuchadnezzar's troubled spirit. Nebuchadnezzar knew beyond question that Daniel's description of the dream and its interpretation were correct. Clearly, Daniel knew his position and expressed respect for Nebuchadnezzar. He acknowledged that God gave Nebuchadnezzar power to rule over everything.

> You, O king, are the king of kings. The God of heaven has given you dominion and power and might and glory; in your hands He has placed mankind and the beasts of the field and the birds of the air. Wherever they live, He has made you ruler over them all. You are that head of gold (Daniel 2:37-38).

This was the beginning of a lifelong trust or bond that grew stronger with time. The second accomplishment of the dream was it planted a seed in Nebuchadnezzar's heart. This made Nebuchadnezzar's heart pliable enough to recognize and even give praise to Daniel's God.

Then King Nebuchadnezzar fell upon his face, and worshipped Daniel, and commanded that they should offer an oblation and sweet odours unto him. The king answered Daniel and said, "Truly your God is a God of gods, and a Lord of kings, and a revealer of secrets, since you could reveal this secret." Then the king promoted Daniel and gave him many great gifts, and made him ruler over the whole province of Babylon and chief of the governors over all the wise men of Babylon (Daniel 2:46-48).

"Nebuchadnezzar honored Daniel and Daniel's God. If Daniel had taken the credit himself, the king would have honored only Daniel. Because Daniel gave God the credit, the king honored both of them. Our acts of love and compassion may impress people, and if we give God credit for our actions, they will want to know more about Him."[42] While the seed planted got choked off, Daniel's efforts were not in vain.

And let us not be weary in well doing; for in due season
we shall reap, if we faint not (Galatians 6:9).

Yes, we often pass the baton or "good work" on to someone else. Scripture bears out that some plant spiritual seeds, some water, and God causes the increase (1 Cor. 3:7). Did you ever think you might be planting seed that you, yourself, will water years down the road? Nebuchadnezzar observed Daniel's humility and awe-inspiring faith in that he never took credit for himself. "He took credit for nothing. He explained he would not have known the dream except God revealed it to him. He gave all the honor and glory to the Lord. He always gave God the glory. When Daniel gave God the glory, even a heathen king wanted to know

---

42. Footnote from Daniel 2:47, *New King James Version: Life Application Study Bible* (United States: Tyndale House Publishers, Incorporated, 1996), 1496.

this God who was so powerful that He could reveal a dream that he had already forgotten."[43]

I thought it relevant, if not poignant, to insert that further along in Daniel's story we see the angel Gabriel telling Daniel he was greatly cherished by heaven.

> At the beginning of the supplications the commandment came forth, and I am come to shew thee; for thou art greatly beloved: therefore understand the matter and consider the vision (Daniel 9:23).

The Hebrew word for "beloved" is *chamad*, which means "precious, to delight in, pleasant." Roughly 400 years later the same angel, Gabriel, used a different word to Mary, soon to be the mother of Jesus, describing how heaven felt about her.

> And the angel came in unto her, and said, Hail, thou that art highly favored, the Lord is with thee; blessed art thou among women (Luke 1:28).

The Greek word for "favored" is *charitoo*, which means to "endue with special honor, to make accepted, to grace, to be highly favored." "Blessed" is the Greek word *eulogeo*, which means "to speak well of, praise," and is taken from *eveu*, which means "good, well done." Translated, I take both messages to mean, "Well done, my good and faithful servants. Almighty God is about to give you a very important message."

Don't we all want to hear that when face to face with God in His kingdom? Well, what was the message? It was the most important message mankind could ever hope to hear—a message pertaining to the birth and death of the Savior of the world. There can be no doubt who the Messiah really is. Imagine Gabriel or any celestial entity telling

---

43. N.W. Hutchings, *Exploring the Book of Daniel*, (Oklahoma City, OK: Hearthstone Publishing, 1990), 37-38.

you a message like that and calling you *Beloved* or *Blessed of God*. Well guess what? God Himself told us personally and directly from His Word, which is "Jesus made flesh" (John 1:14). "Beloved" in the Greek is *agapetos* built from the root word *agape*. We already know *agape* is "to love with affection, dearly." Throughout the New Testament true believers and followers in Christ are referred to as God's beloved. God loves us with His kind of love, an affection that He holds very, very dear. This is huge!

Now, if the devil is worth his weight in salt, he will remind you of the many "terrible" things you've done. You are not loved like the rest because of what you've done—or didn't do. Please give God more credit than that. Remember, He chose you before the foundation of the world. In other words, He chose you before you were even born.

> For He chose us in Him before the creation of the world
> to be holy and blameless in his sight (Ephesians 1:4).

Christ knew every sin you would ever commit, but He still loves you with an agape love. Where you "rest" for all of eternity is up to you. P.S. It is not a noble thing to not forgive yourself. If you have repented and committed the remainder of your life to Him, He forgave you. You are not greater than Him. Are you?

A couple of short years later, King Nebuchadnezzar had another disturbing dream, unlike the former dream—a remarkable, telescopic magnification of traveling through time to view the forecast of mankind. This new dream was about him. Hopefully, I have aroused your interest enough to provoke an independent study on Nebuchadnezzar's dreams. It surely would not be a waste of time. Right now, I prefer to focus on the relational interaction between bondservant and bondsman, i.e. Daniel and Nebuchadnezzar. It is interesting to note that Nebuchadnezzar chose to write this piece of history himself, specifically Daniel 4:1-18, 34-37. Daniel inserted these verses at both the beginning and the end of chapter four after Nebuchadnezzar's incredible seven-year experience of acting like an ox. The Lord gave Daniel the interpretation that Nebuchadnezzar so desperately sought. But instead of staying humble and giving thanks to Daniel and Daniel's God, he allowed himself to enter into pride whereby he was severely chastened.

Remember, Daniel did not start to write the book of Daniel until 536 B.C., 22 years after Nebuchadnezzar passed at the not so old age of 66 or 67, making Daniel close to 87 years old. Therefore, it was easy for him to insert Nebuchadnezzar's words into his story. Or was it? Daniel didn't have to credit the deceased king or for that matter do anything for him ever again. Yet something inside Daniel wanted to tell Nebuchadnezzar's story as Nebuchadnezzar wanted it told. Only God can see and read our hearts. I believe over the 43 years Daniel knew him, something was stirring on the inside. He, no doubt, experienced numerous emotions, the one constant being the agape love he had for his heavenly Father. Along the way, Daniel saw how God was using him to soften probably one of the toughest and hardest men who ever lived. He used Nebuchadnezzar's own words to expose the majesty and splendor of a sinner turned saint.

Nebuchadnezzar started with unabashedly praising God to the entire world about every aspect he could think of, i.e. His signs, wonders, kingdom, and dominion. The passages show Nebuchadnezzar humbled to the core and letting everyone who "dwell[s] in all the earth" know what happened. Let's stop right here. This next part is unequivocally humiliating. He had a scary dream and woke up troubled—so much so that he issued a non-threatening decree to all "wise men" to make known its interpretation, whereupon "at last Daniel came" to save the day. It's interesting to note that no punitive action would be administered if no one was able to interpret the dream. Instead, he goes on to repeat the word of the "holy ones, that the Most High rules in the kingdom of men, gives it to whomever He will, and sets over it the lowest of men." The reason for this will soon be apparent. Personally, I believe these words stayed deep inside his spirit while he experienced a mental disorder some call boanthropy, an aberration in which a person tempo-rarily believes himself to be a cow or ox and proceeds to act like one.

Daniel didn't launch into an explanation as he had with the previous vision. This time he was "astonished" and "troubled" so much so that the king had to encourage him to continue. The word for "astonished" in Hebrew is *shmam*. It means "stun or stupefy." It can also mean "dev-astate." As American citizens in the 21st century, it takes a lot to stupefy or stun us. *Devastate* has a whole different connotation. That requires emotion that is reserved for those we really care about. It's not a volun-tary thing. It comes out of true shock and inner displeasure. *Troubled* comes from the Hebrew word *behal* corresponding with *bahal*. This means "to terrify inwardly, palpitate, be alarmed, agitate, afraid, amaze, dismay, and even vex."

These are very strong emotions with physical repercussions. How can anyone have such an intensely powerful reaction to news straight from God if they either don't know or don't care about a person deeply? Nebuchadnezzar already sensed Daniel's feelings of sincerity, which strengthened the bond that began years ago. Then Daniel confirmed his feelings: "My lord, may the dream concern those who hate you, and its interpretation concern your enemies!" (Dan. 4:19). The antonym of hate is love and enemy is friend. This kind of friendship love is called *phileo,* which condensed means "brotherly love, brotherly kindness, love of the brethren." One can no longer question the strength of the bond between Nebuchadnezzar and Daniel; instead, they can identify it.

"How could Daniel be so deeply grieved at the fate of Nebuchadnezzar-the king who was responsible for the destruction of Daniel's home and nation? Daniel had for-given Nebuchadnezzar and so God was able to use Dan-iel. Very often when we have been wronged by someone, we find it difficult to forget the past. We may even be glad when the person suffers. Forgiveness means putting the past behind us. Can you serve someone who has mistreated you? Ask God to help you forgive, forget, and love. God may use you in an extraordinary way in that person's life."[44]

Daniel proceeded to explain the dream and proffer an interpretation. He then went on to describe the personification of a great tree that supplied sustenance to all living beings on the earth. Suddenly this great tree of provision was chopped to the ground, leaving only a stump that was to be bound with a band of iron and bronze. The iron and bronze signified future kingdoms that would surely replace Nebuchadnezzar's magnificent yet worldly kingdom. Daniel went on to speak of the decree of the Most High God, that Nebuchadnezzar would be driven from men and dwell among the beasts in the field, eating grass just like one of the oxen for seven years until he knew "that the Most High rules in the kingdom of men, and gives it to whomever He chooses" (Dan. 4:25).

Human stomachs have difficulty digesting grass and leaves. Animals don't because of a process called rumination, requiring multiple stomach chambers. Grass also contains a lot of silica, which is so abrasive it can literally wear your teeth down to a nub. Grazing animals have teeth that are adaptable and continually grow. God knew it would take Nebuchadnezzar seven whole years to realize this. God knows all things from the beginning to the end. There are many scriptures to support this—Isaiah 46:10; 48:3; Revelation 1:8; 22:13, to name a few. You've heard there are no coincidences, right? The number seven means completion.

Now one of the most interesting things in this whole story happened—Daniel witnessed to Nebuchadnezzar a second time. He actually witnessed salvation "Old Testament" style.

---

44. Footnote from Daniel 4:19, *New King James Version: Life Application Study Bible* (United States: Tyndale House Publishers, Incorporated, 1996), 1500-1501.

> Break off your sins by being righteous, and your iniqui-
> ties by showing mercy to the poor. Perhaps there may be
> a lengthening of your prosperity (Daniel 4:27).

Righteous is taken from *tsidqah,* which means "beneficence or
doing good, producing acts of kindness and charity (love)." *Tsidqah*
comes from *tsadaq,* which means "to cleanse or clear self, physically
or spiritually." *Mercy* is taken from *chanan,* which means "to entreat,
make supplication, implore, beseech, have pity upon, pray." My break-
down: Pray and confess that you believe the Most High God is the one
true God. Petition Him to forgive your iniquities and cleanse your soul.
Be kind to the poor and less fortunate, and the Lord God will reward
you greatly. Paul said it similarly, but in terms we can understand better,
618 years later after the divine union with humanity in the Person of
Jesus Christ.

> The word is near you, in your mouth and in your heart
> (that is, the word of faith which we preach): if you con-
> fess with your mouth the Lord Jesus and believe in your
> heart that God has raised Him from the dead, you will be
> saved. For with the heart one believes unto righteousness,
> and with the mouth confession is made unto salvation."
> For the scripture says, "whoever believes on Him will
> not be put to shame." For there is no distinction between
> Jew and Greek (Chaldean) for the same Lord over all is
> rich to all who call upon Him. "For whoever calls on the
> name of the Lord shall be saved" (Romans 10:8-13).

Speaking of mercy, God was extremely merciful to Nebuchadnezzar. He prophesied to him through Daniel 12 months before speaking to
him in an audible voice, calling him by name.

> While the word was in the king's mouth, there fell a
> voice from heaven, saying, O King Nebuchadnezzar,

137

to thee it is spoken; The kingdom is departed from thee
(Daniel 4:31).

Then, God gave him a second chance—after seven years wet and
munching grass, despite the body being incapable of digesting it and
the teeth not staying intact for that long. All this time, his kingdom was
secure and his men remained loyal and gladly accepted him back once
he recovered his senses. You might think this not fair because God has
not gone to such an extent for many others. Whether God has or not,
we should understand that Nebuchadnezzar was God's instrument of
destruction for many years. It is God's prerogative to have mercy on
whom He will. If He chooses to offer this great mercy to His servant,
who are we to question?

> And at the end of the days I Nebuchadnezzar lifted up
> mine eyes unto heaven, and mine understanding returned
> unto me, and I blessed the most High, and I praised and
> honoured him that liveth forever, whose dominion is an
> everlasting dominion, and his kingdom is from generation
> to generation. At the same time my reason returned unto
> me; and for the glory of my kingdom, mine honour and
> brightness returned unto me; my counselors and my lords
> sought unto me; and I was established in my kingdom, and
> excellent majesty was added unto me (Daniel 4:34,36).

Through Daniel's actions and faithfulness, he showed God's love to
Nebuchadnezzar. It was Daniel's integrity and humility that won him
over. Witnessing is an act of obedience as commissioned by the Lord
Jesus Christ. It is an act of mercy. It is bestowing on another what they
do not deserve. It is pure agape love for the One who commissioned us
and who by redemption did not give us what we do deserve. Every time
we witness, there is the great possibility that the individual will receive
the seed in good soil either then or somewhere down the road. When we
witness, we no longer function or act solely from our mind or emotions.

We reach deep down into our spirits as a people of God, the true royalty of God, the spiritual seed of Abraham we were created to be.

What if the situation had been reversed? Could you put aside bitterness and resentment? In your suffering, could you keep the love? Only the love of God can do that. If Daniel could do it, with the Spirit of God in him, so can you and I. We can let the love of God flow through us. With an uncertain future ahead, there may come a time when you will be called upon, like our brother of over two and a half millennia ago, to "witness" to the enemy. Remember, if you surrender everything to God, you become ambassadors for the Most High. This time, Daniel's witnessing to Nebuchadnezzar yielded great fruit. He watered the seed planted a decade earlier. If this isn't love, what is? King Nebuchadnezzar's final words loudly proclaimed how Daniel's God was now his God:

> Now I, Nebuchadnezzar, praise and extol and honor the
> King of heaven, all of whose works are truth, and His
> ways just and those who walk in pride He is able to abase
> (Daniel 4:37).

We hear no more from this great and mighty king after chapter 4. I believe because of Daniel's perseverance and forgiving heart, we will see Nebuchadnezzar in heaven. Imagine walking along the golden road and seeing Daniel and Nebuchadnezzar sitting by the hearth chatting. That's the power of forgiveness in action.

Chapter Eight

Demoniac to Evangelist: The Man from Gadara

I n today's world of horror movies and portrayals of demonized individuals, the story of the demoniac from Gadara might cause us to
shudder as we read the account of this poor soul. Enter stage right—
his Deliverer. Jesus. A man totally polluted with demons of the worst
kind had but one thing to live for—the tiny hope that he would one day
be rescued from himself. It was the only thing that kept him alive. He
would recognize Him whom he loved when he saw Him.

At the outset I want to give the man from Gadara a fictitious name
because his name is not revealed in the Bible. I realize this is terribly
presumptuous, but I want to humanize, not demonize, him. An actual
name may open us up to the kind of empathy needed to feel something
for him. How can we even begin to relate to the love Jesus had for him
unless we open up our hearts? I picture him as big, burly, very strong,
yet scared, lonely, and in pain. There he was alone in the middle of the
tombs (imagine being in a scary graveyard in the pitch black of night)
with no food, no clothes, no shelter, no companions, no hope, shackled
and in chains. Because he reminds me of an almost-grown male bear
prematurely ripped from his family, I want to call him Teddy.

We know next to nothing about Teddy. Out of nowhere, we meet this naked man living under horrible conditions, but for good reason. He was considered a danger to himself and others. He was known for crying out, shrieking, and screaming day and night while beating, bruising, and cutting himself with stones. He was labeled insane, out of his mind, an insane hermit, a mad man, a demoniac, and more. Just because he was chained for "safety" purposes doesn't mean he was insane. He wasn't—at least, not all the time. Only when the demons "seized" him. *Seized* means "control, manipulate, make him do things, to take force or lay hold suddenly or forcibly, capture, to attack or overwhelm physically, to possess overwhelmingly." Yet, nowhere do I find that Teddy tried to harm another human being. Isn't that interesting?

> Then they sailed to the country of the Gadarenes, which is opposite Galilee. And when He stepped out on the land, there met Him a certain man from the city who had demons for a long time. For He had commanded the unclean spirit to come out of the man. For it had often seized him, and he was kept under guard, bound with chains and shackles; and he broke the bonds and was driven by the demon into the wilderness (Luke 8:26-27, 29).

Once free, the demons would "drive" him out of the tombs and into the mountains or desert. He refused to stay shackled.

> For he had been bound often with shackles for the feet, and handcuffs, but the handcuffs [of light] chains he wrenched apart, and the shackles he rubbed and ground together and broke in pieces; and no one had strength enough to restrain or tame him (Mark 5:4).

Gadara is five miles southeast of the Chinneret or Sea of Galilee and three miles from the river Hiromax, now called Yarmuk. The most interesting ruins at Gadara are the tombs, which are very numerous in the cliffs around the city. The Greek word for "tomb" is *mnemeion,* meaning "grave." They are cut in the solid rock, being rooms ten to twenty feet square, and some larger, with small recesses for bodies, the doors being stone, turning on stone hinges.[45] Approximately 200 people still lie at rest here.

I had difficulty imagining Jesus and His disciples trekking five miles and bumping into Teddy along the way or the herd of swine running six miles down the cliff and falling into the sea. What cliff and what sea? Scripture doesn't say it happened that way. Teddy saw Him and raced to Him. It didn't make sense until I found this. Kursi—a city on the eastern shore of the Sea of Galilee. Gergasai and Gadara are used interchangeably. It was called the country of the Gergesenes and here, the Bible says, Jesus cast out the demons. It was known as Kursi in Jewish sources and Gergasai in other sources where it is mentioned as the location where the herd of swine had drowned.[46] The country or the Gergesenes is located southeast of the Sea of Galilee, near the town of Gadara, one of the most important cites of the region. Gadara was a member of the Decapolis. These 10 cities with independent governments were largely inhabited by Gentiles, which explains the herd of swine. The Jews did not raise pigs because pigs were considered unclean and thus unfit to eat.[47]

While I superimposed a name on the man from Gadara, I wouldn't dare presume how he got in this situation. Instead, I will briefly expound upon ways demon possession can occur—many of which are mind-altering. Sorcery is a big one. Opening a door to the kingdom of darkness gives Satan a foothold like no other. Often, he wedges the door open

45. William Smith, *Smith's Bible Dictionary Complete Concordance Revised Ed.* (Nashville, TN: Holman Bible Publishers, 1991) 110.

46. "Gergesa," Bible History Maps, accessed July 9, 2022, https://Bible-history.com/geography/gergesa.

47. Footnote from Matthew 8:28, *New King James Version: Life Application Study Bible* (United States: Tyndale House Publishers, Incorporated, 1996), pg. 1691.

slowly so he can open it wider and wider over time. It may start with a seemingly innocent Ouija board or exciting game like "Dungeons and Dragons." Then one may move up to palm reading or some other kind of future-telling practice. There are many of them, each hold their own promise of fascination. Over time the opening gets wider; eventually full possession can take over leading the naïve but very seduced person into believing and doing awful things.

Let's review several more types of dark magic. The first we'll define is witchcraft. "Witchcraft—an act of employing sorcery (the use of power gained from the assistance or control of spirits) especially with malevolent intent, and the exercise of supernatural powers and alleged intercourse with the devil or a familiar [spirit]."[48] Additionally, "Fortune telling is the practice of predicting information about a person's life. The scope of fortune telling is in principle identical with the practice of divination. The difference is that divination is the term used for predictions considered part of a religious ritual, invoking deities or spirits, while the term fortune telling implies a less serious or formal setting, even one of popular culture." Common methods or means used for fortune telling or powers of suggestion include astrology, pendulum reading, tea leaves, crystal spheres, contact with or distance from objects, amulets, axes on posts, "lucky" charms, omens, pentagrams, superstition, and paranormal activities.[49] Next, sorcery "is the deliberate employment of magic rites, the use of spell or mechanical aids in the attempt to bring in results. It can be used either for a good or an evil purpose." Practices of sorcery may include rituals, spells, chants, incantations, Satanism, animal/child sacrifices, and fortune telling.[50]

---

48. "Definitions for Witchcraft," US National Library of Medicine, Definitions.net, accessed July 11, 2022, https://www.definitions.net/definition/witchcraft.

49. "Fortune-Telling," *Wikipedia*, last modified May 12, 2022, https://en.wikipedia.org/wiki/Fortune-telling.

50. "What is Witchcraft?" Opoku Onyinah, The Henry Center for Theological Understanding, published April 10, 2015, https://henrycenter.tiu.edu/2015/04/what-is-witchcraft/.

Make no mistake about it—this stuff is powerful and real. (Please note that this paragraph is graphic and tough to read. You may want to skip over it.) Just recently I received a petition from Animal Recovery Mission (ARM) based out of Miami to send to the Governor to stop black magic gangs. Haitian, Cuban, and other communities that practice these vile pagan rituals are torturing and slaughtering dogs, cats, goats, sheep, and even horses. There is a ceremony known as "crucifixion" where all four limbs are broken, then tied to a cross and a wooden stake is forced into its mouth to stop the animal from defending itself. This is a five-day long ceremony. Moreover, there are other forms of sacrifice in which animals are left in macabre pits then beheaded while still alive. As graphic as these descriptions are, at least they didn't include any pictures. There are animal rescues located throughout the country. Just go to the Better Business Bureau and type in the category and location nearest you. These brave undercover investigators use sophisticated surveillance and tracking technology to hunt, infiltrate the voodoo ceremonies, and shut them down. A contribution of some kind will no doubt be much appreciated for the rescue and care of these innocent animals.

I had a neighbor who fell in love with a married man. She was so excited because she was going to a local fair and planned on getting her fortune told. I knew enough from my parents to discourage her from doing this. I warned her bad things could come of it. But no, she had to find out if Joe would really leave his wife and marry her like he promised. Afterward she was never the same. The fortune teller told her something that turned her amiable personality into full-blown depression for the rest of the time I lived there. This was long enough to learn that Joe never left his wife up to the day he died of a sudden heart attack. If the sorcerer or sorceress is legitimate, they are possessed with a spirit of divination. A familiar spirit sent to spy on families reveals information to the spirit of divination that provides just enough detail to make the soothsayer, diviner, fortune teller, voodoo or medicine man, witch, psychic, whatever you want to call them seem for real. Sometimes it only takes once, as in the case of my neighbor, or at the very least it is enough to lure them back to the source over and over again until it escalates.

> Regard not them that have familiar spirits, neither seek after wizards, to be defiled by them: I am the Lord your God (Leviticus 19:31).

> And the soul that turneth after such as have familiar spirits, and after wizards, to go a whoring after them, I will even set my face against that soul, and will cut him off from among his people (Leviticus 20:6).

> There shall not be found among you anyone that maketh his son or his daughter to pass through the fire [burn alive], or that useth divination, or an observer of times, or an enchanter, or a witch. Or a charmer, or a consulter with familiar spirits, or a wizard, or a necromancer [to summon or entreat spirits of the dead for purposes of magically revealing the future or influencing the course of events]. For all that do these things are an abomination unto the Lord: and because of these abominations the Lord thy God doth drive them out from before thee. Thou shalt be perfect with the Lord thy God (Deuteronomy 18:10-13).

Idolatry and witchcraft have brought many a king and kingdom down.

> And the spirit of Egypt shall fail in the midst thereof: and I will destroy the counsel thereof: and they shall seek to the idols, and to the charmers, and to them that have familiar spirits, and to the wizards. And the Egyptians will I give over into the hand of a cruel lord; and a fierce king shall rule over them, saith the Lord, the Lord of hosts (Isaiah 19:3-4).

King Saul, the first in Israel, could have maintained his kingship in perpetuity but instead lost that distinguished honor, his life, and three of his sons all in the same battle because of his disobedience.

> And Samuel said to Saul, "You have done foolishly. You have not kept the commandment of the Lord your God, which He commanded you. For now the Lord would have established your kingdom over Israel forever. But now your kingdom shall not continue. The Lord has sought for Himself a man after His own heart, and the Lord has commanded him to be commander over His people, because you have not kept what the Lord commanded you"(1 Samuel 13:13-14).

> So Saul died, and his three sons, and all his house died together (1 Chronicles 10:6).

> So Saul died for his transgression which he committed against the Lord, even against the word of the Lord, which he kept not, and also for asking counsel of one that had a familiar spirit, to enquire of it; And enquired not of the Lord: therefore He slew him, and turned the kingdom unto David the son of Jesse (1 Chronicles 10:13-14).

Years of living a lifestyle contrary to the Word of God results in a hardened heart. Stubbornness and rebellion become an established disposition that more or less dictates your every point of view. This is a dangerous stance because changing your views or openness to new ideas or beliefs gets increasingly difficult and easier for Satan to open the door a little wider. This is exactly what happened to Saul.

> For rebellion is as the sin of witchcraft, and stubbornness is as iniquity and idolatry. Because thou has rejected the

word of the Lord, he hath also rejected thee (Saul) from
being king (1 Samuel 15:23).

Admitting you're wrong is no easy matter, especially if it's been
over the course of a lifetime. Satan will continue to use the same old
tricks, leaning on your weaknesses, possibly the same weaknesses or
sins as those of your parents and grandparents and generations before
them. Desensitization is subtle. You may feel guilty at first, but repeated
sin results in spiritual numbness or hard-hardheartedness. Don't worry,
Satan is more than willing to wait. He hates us all simply for being
created by God. Originally, he thought he could outrank God if he won
enough support. Once he was thrown out of heaven, along with all of his
supporters (one third of the angels), his motive for every evil deed has
been hatred and revenge. Because his time is growing short he is step-
ping up his game. Just turn to the news on any social platform. Meanwhile, God gets blamed when all along it was the person themselves
making very poor choices. No one can say that God hasn't warned us.

And the great dragon was cast down, the old serpent,
he that is called the Devil and Satan, the deceiver of
the whole world; he was cast down to the earth, and his
angels were cast down with him (Revelation 12:9).

Therefore rejoice, Oh heavens, and you that dwell in
them. Woe for the earth and for the sea: because the devil
has gone to you, having great wrath, knowing that he has
but a short time (Revelation 12:12).

Very early in my career I worked with juvenile offenders. My job
was to teach them how to integrate back into society utilizing "music in
special education" as a means to effectively equip and contribute to their
overall well-being. One such student was always challenging me with
questions. One particularly difficult question went something like, "The
Bible says not to curse the Holy Spirit. I did anyway. Does that mean

I'm going to hell?" I answered that with, "As long as you feel remorse, God will forgive you." He got paroled, then murdered someone shortly afterward. It would seem his heart only got harder and harder. I never saw or heard from him again, but I wonder where he is today both physically and especially spiritually.

> And sin, when it is finished, bringeth forth death (James 1:15b).

People aren't born demon-possessed, but it can happen when people tamper with the dark arts. Possession can happen so gradually that often family and neighbors don't even see it coming. The Hebrew word for sorcery is *kesheph,* which means magic or witchcraft. A similar meaning is applied to the Greek word *pharmakia,* which has a double meaning: 1) sorcery. 2) the misuse of drugs; a medicine, drug, poison, philter (a potion, drug, or charm held to have the power to arouse sexual passion) charm, enchantment; a harmful or healing medicine, a healing or poisonous herb, poisonous potion, magic potion; Drugs are a byproduct of sorcery.

> Now the works of the flesh are manifest, which are these; Adultery, fornication, uncleanness, lasciviousness, idolatry, witchcraft, hatred, variance [dissension, dispute], emulations [envious rivalry], wrath, seditions [insurrection against lawful authority], heresies [one who dissents from an accepted belief or doctrine], envyings, murders, drunkenness, revelings, and such like: of the which I tell you before, as I have told you in time past, that they which do such things shall not inherit the kingdom of God (Galatians 5:19-21).

Satan is very intelligent and always on the lookout for the most vulnerable. He is an opportunist waiting for another chance to strike. An example I would like to provide is the song "Helter Skelter" recorded on the White Album by The Beatles in 1969. A man by the name of

Charles Manson became fascinated with this song and totally twisted its meaning. Manson thought it was a prediction of racial civil war between blacks and whites. Paul McCartney, its composer, claimed to have created this piece in order to make a loud and screaming noise about the rise and particularly the fall of the Roman Empire. *Helter-skelter* means "confusion, disorder, and haphazard." Satan is the author of confusion. *Merriam-Webster's Collegiate Dictionary, Tenth Edition* breaks down *helter-skelter* into synonyms by adverbs—amuck, berserk, frantically, frenziedly, madly, wildly—and by adjectives—overhasty, rash, headlong, Gadarene, which is characteristic of Gadara. Wait, what? While the actual word *Gadara* is not used in the Bible, we know that a Gadarene was an inhabitant of Gadara. Gadarene means "moving rapidly, and without control, headlong," taken from the incident of swine racing headlong into the sea.

Are you starting to see a pattern here? I'll ask you this again a little later. Anything to do with evil can be traced back to Satan. Throughout this story, Teddy, my neighbor, my student, and for so many others, there is a connection. A stealthy and insidious thread of persuasive evil lurks in everyone's story. No one is immune, but there is a way to overcome (1 John 4:4).

> You are of God, little children, and have overcome them, because He who is in you is greater than he who is in the world. The thief comes only to steal and kill and destroy; I have come that they may have life, and have it to the full (John 10:10 NIV).

Already you might be thinking, "How could Charles Manson have ever been anything but evil?" He claimed one of his biggest influences was the song "Helter Skelter." Books, documentaries, and a movie about the story of the Manson family cult murders shook the world in the late sixties. The book *Helter Skelter,* written by Vincent Bugliosi and Curt Gentry, depicted nine brutal slayings in four different locations the summer of 1969 (even though Manson is suspected of killing 35). At the age of 12, he could no longer live with his mother, an alcoholic and prostitute. He went from foster homes to living on the street where he committed petty crimes then wound up in one reform school after another, which led to one prison after another. As a young adult, he married a couple of times and began to study various cult religions. He turned to drugs and decided to start a quasi-commune or cult family of his own based in California. He influenced his family of 100 followers to use habitual drugs such as LSD and hallucinogenic mushrooms and had young impressionable girls willing to do absolutely anything for their "new messiah." A series of circumstances such as I have described left the door to his soul wide open for humanity's greatest enemy, Satan. He became "pathologically deluded into believing he [was destined to be] the harbinger of doom" for this planet. Initially his big goal in life was to massacre Hollywood's elite and beautiful because the world of showbiz rejected him. Then his goals evolved to shock value in order to make people sit up and take notice. After 40 years of imprisonment leading to his demise, Manson left behind a legacy of probation reports describing him as suffering from, among other things, "psychic trauma."[51]

Another immediate but subtle spiritual threat that we often don't consider is technology and/or virtual reality. I believe hypnosis, dark movies, media containing sexually explicit and excessive violence, art defying God or promoting evil, and other types of mind-altering substances, shock treatment, and traumatic experiences have influenced many to do or get others to do ungodly things. Defense attorneys build their cases on the idea that these influences have caused mental illnesses. I don't say these are the only ways Satan can gain possession, but these are areas from which God warns us to stay away. A combination of these sins can be deadly.

---

51. "Charles Manson", Biography.com Editors, published March 15, 2018, https://www.biography.com/crime-figure/charles-manson.

Psychiatric wards, especially those housing the criminally insane, along with prisons and death row have their fair share of demented spirits or possessed people. I used to do volunteer work at these types of state facilities. I walked through the wards, accompanied by staff, and would see people rocking back and forth, talking to the voices they heard, the remains of urination or defecation on the floor, making hideous sounds. Demon possession is not in the *Diagnostic and Statistical Manual of Mental Disorders* (DSM) published by the American Psychiatric Association. The majority of these patients are heavily drugged to quell their urge to escape or hurt someone. I believe many are suffering from demonic oppression. Satan will use anything he can get away with. We need to be cautious of the choices we make and what we let influence our spirits and our minds. He is always ready to attack; thus, we can't underestimate him.

Let me give you a more specific example. I used to lead a prison ministry. Two teams would meet at the detention center in Mercerville, New Jersey every Tuesday night. The men would go to an all-male tier, the women a female tier. We would take Bibles to give to the inmates. I noticed this one woman was always locked up in her tiny nine-by-nine cell. She was never allowed to join us in the designated area for those who wanted to attend Bible study. This one particular night as I was standing outside her cell, she asked me for a Bible. Naturally, I handed her one through the bars and she immediately threw it in a big black plastic bag. Trying not to upset her, as she would spit on me if I did, I asked her what was in the bag. She explained she was collecting Bibles. When she saw her baby girl in heaven she would give them to her. She went on to explain how she threw her daughter into the windshield of an oncoming car just to save her from this terrible world. She said it just as calmly as if she had just rocked her baby to sleep as any loving mother would do. Her story was confirmed. Hours later I finally stopped shaking.

This next story will show how abuse is evil and can open up doors to dark spirits, thereby taking a toll on a person mentally. This story for me is personal. During elementary school days I had a classmate named Gary. At first, he teased me a lot until finally one day we became friends. He even lived near my house and he came over to ride horses with me as I lived on a small ranch. Gary was a foster child shoved from one home to another, some not so nice. Because a very bad thing occurred in that last home, Gary and all the kids were displaced. Once he graduated high school (a different one from mine) he joined the army. We lost touch once he moved, and I basically forgot about him until it came on national news that Gary, now honorably discharged, was in a standoff with the police shooting at them outside of his mother's upstairs window. The end result was three cops were killed and another paralyzed from the neck down until he died years later from his injuries.

Gary was locked up (and still is) in a forensics unit for the criminally insane. I couldn't believe it! My friend Gary. How could it be? Because I had volunteer status it was not that difficult to visit him. He was drugged and calm and still remembered me. We had several visits. Eventually he opened up about why he was there. He did not deny what he had done but justified it. In his mind he had lived many lives before. In each one of them he was badly beaten and abused. He wasn't sure who hurt him; it could easily have been those cops. That's when I knew no one was safe alone with him again.

The next time I visited him I gave him a book on Christianity versus reincarnation and we prayed. He asked Jesus to forgive him and to be his Lord and Savior. He told me he didn't think Jesus could ever forgive him for what he did. I told him nothing was impossible for God. The very next day he went to his weekly AA meeting, which he liked to attend because it got him out of the building once a week for an hour. He asked me to join him at the next one because he wanted to show me something. It was there he showed me an amazing sign that he had never seen before hanging from the mantle. All it said was, "*I forgive you.*" It moved him deeply. He didn't think God forgiving him was possible, not even for God, but now he had peace like he had never known.

> Be anxious for nothing, but in everything by prayer
> and supplication, with thanksgiving, let your requests
> be made known to God; and the peace of God, which
> surpasses all understanding, will guard your hearts and
> minds through Christ Jesus (Philippians 4:6-7).

You see how the devil can get a foothold? After years of abuse in foster homes and no doubt PTSD from his experience in Vietnam, Gary came back and committed an unthinkable crime yet totally justified it in his suffering mind. That wasn't enough for Satan; now he used a new torment—mental torment. He wanted to destroy what was left of what was once an ordinary kid running around the playground.

I'll ask it again—are you beginning to sense a pattern with the enemy of old? God wants us to be armed against any spiritual attack. He wants us to use the authority we have been given in Christ. He does not want us to be afraid. He wants us to listen. He told us that fear is a spirit. That's right, it's just another one of Satan's minions. He uses them as a scare tactic to keep you under his control and not trusting God.

> For God hath not given us a spirit of fear; but of power,
> and of love, and of a sound mind (2 Timothy 1:7).

God, the Greater One, has given us a sound mind, a sane mind, a good mind.

You might think that once you make a decision for Christ, Satan will become your enemy and now you'll be asking for trouble. Are you created? Remember that Satan hates you merely because you exist, because God created you, and because He loves you. When you make a decision for Christ you become a threat to him. He knows he can no longer control you, but you have to read the Bible and learn how to protect yourself. If you know how to defend yourself, you can keep him as far from you and your loved ones as the east is from the west.

Finally, my brethren, be strong in the Lord and in the power of His might. Put on the whole armor of God, that you may be able to stand against the wiles of the devil. For we do not wrestle against flesh and blood, but against principalities, against powers, against the rulers of the darkness of this age, against spiritual hosts of wickedness in the heavenly places. Therefore, take up the whole armor of God, that you may be able to withstand in the evil day, and having done all, to stand (Ephesians 6:10-13).

For the weapons of our warfare are not carnal but mighty in God for pulling down strongholds (2 Corinthians 10:4).

Jesus protected Himself. After 40 days of being tempted in the wilderness, having eaten nothing, Satan came at Him with three temptations. Each time Jesus answered with "It is written," but in response to the second temptation in which Satan offered all the kingdoms of the world along with their power and glory, He added something. This time Jesus said, "Get thee behind me, Satan: for it is written…." The more you learn the Word, the greater your faith will be to use your greatest weapon, the Word of God.

So, then faith comes by hearing, and hearing by the Word of God (Romans 10:17).

Lastly, Jesus spoke these words directly to Satan; therefore, He did not have to credit a higher power for this authority. Jesus said greater works than these we will do that believe in Him. He also emphasized using His name and asking the Father in His name. You have authority over the devil but always, always use the name of Jesus.

Verily, verily, I say unto you, He that believeth on Me, the works that I do shall he do also; and greater works than these shall he do; because I go unto my Father. And whatsoever you shall ask in My name, that will I do, that the Father may be glorified in the Son. If you shall ask anything in My name, I will do it (John 14:12-14 KJV).

Behold, I give you the authority to trample on serpents and scorpions, and over all the power of the enemy, and nothing shall by any means hurt you (Luke 10:19).

Jesus cast many evil spirits from people throughout the Bible. There's an example of a little boy who apparently went into fits because of demonic possession, and thankfully his father knew enough to lay him at the feet of the Mighty One. One demon alone can cause much damage. It can cause a person to lose his voice, sight, and hearing, and even appear to have suicidal tendencies with no apparent injury or deformity anywhere on or in their body. Beyond mental illness and fits of rage, demons can also bring sickness and other physical ailments.

Let's get back to Teddy. He was probably afraid of his own shadow at this point, cold and alone (the average temperature being 53 degrees during the day), with no clothing to cover his bleeding body, never knowing when the hideous creatures inside him would attack and take over. Honestly, none of us can fathom how it must have felt to have thousands of demons invade. Teddy had a multitude of demons inside him yet he walked, talked, and fought to stay alive. Something inside him wouldn't give up. Like Jesus, he was one of the strongest men who ever lived because he hung on. Jesus used every ounce of His being to not call twelve legions of angels to get Him down from that cross. He waited for merciful death. With a similar passion, Teddy waited for merciful life. He may have thought there was no hope for him, but something inside his heart wouldn't let go. Something inside him kept him from jumping over the cliff. He somehow knew deep down that salvation was on the way and worth waiting for.

Then Jesus arrived. There is every indication that Jesus crossed the entire Kinneret (which is over eight miles wide and normally two hours by modern boat, but because of a tremendous storm it took much longer) for one reason—to rescue Teddy. To Him, Teddy wasn't some fierce, hideous monster—he was the leading character in the parable of the lost sheep. The Lord seeks men after His own heart. King or beggar, it makes no difference. Jesus loves you just the same.

> Suppose one of you has a hundred sheep and loses one of them. Does he not leave the ninety-nine in the open country and go after the lost sheep until he finds it? (Luke 15:4 NIV)

> For the eyes of the Lord run to and fro throughout the whole earth, to show Himself strong on behalf of those whose heart is loyal to Him (2 Chronicles 16:9).

Jesus sought after Teddy and his willing heart. Scripture reveals Teddy saw Him from afar among the tombs. I can only imagine Teddy looking beyond where he was very possibly chained up at the time. He immediately recognized Him for whom he had been waiting for years. He started running, dragging one foot in front of another, getting heavier with each step and possibly tripping a few times because of the fetters and rocks. He had to get there before the demons seized him. Thanks be to the grace of God, Teddy made it to the boat that held Jesus and His disciples in time to call Him "The Most High God" before the demons took over.

What commotion. Everyone and everything was panicking except Jesus and Teddy. This was their moment. This was that moment when a man realizes he is in the presence of greatness. This was that moment when he knew he was totally lost without a Savior, and that Savior is Jesus Christ. This was the most beautiful and poignant moment in a person's life when God met human and human met God. This was mankind's defining moment. This is why living in the natural is worth every bit of any suffering you may experience because you have the opportunity to merge with the supernatural and have your destiny marked forever. This is where I envy Teddy. He got to see and worship Jesus face to face, even though it only lasted for a few minutes. Jesus already knew Teddy's heart.

> When he saw Jesus from afar, he ran and worshiped Him (Mark 5:6).

Upon approaching Teddy, Jesus wasted no time casting out the unclean spirit with a word. Something unusual this time—other than to just rebuke it with a word, He asked it its name. The spirits gave their answer: "Legion, for we are many." Several sources indicate a legion can consist of 1,000 to 6,200 demons. A legion was known to be the principle unit of the Roman army consisting of 3,000 to 6,000 foot soldiers plus cavalry. Every resource I turned to had a different number, so I decided to settle on Merriam-Webster's expanded definition of "a very large number; a multitude."

The moment Jesus and His disciples landed, He cast out the unclean spirits from a bloody, filthy, and smelly man kneeling at His feet worshiping Him. The demons had begged to be released into the swine and met their fate. Jesus obliged Legion and cast them into 2,000 pigs (making that a minimum of 2,000 demons in Teddy) that ran wildly down the steep embankment into the sea. The herdsmen ran to the town and stirred up enough people to come and gawk at Jesus, the disciples, and Teddy. The begging continued. The townspeople begged Jesus to leave because they just lost their livelihood, and Teddy begged Jesus to take him with Him. Strangely, Jesus rejected Teddy's petition. Jesus had a bigger plan. Rarely blessings come in tiny packages. Usually, they are sprinkled or rippled all the way across the proverbial lake. You see, Teddy was a Gentile. He would be rejected by the yet unbelieving Jews, not because he was a former demoniac but simply because he was not a Jew. Ministering first to the Jews was Jesus' primary goal. Others were chosen after Him to fulfill that mission.

These twelve Jesus sent out with the following instruction: Do not go among the gentiles or enter any town of the Samaritans. Go rather to the lost sheep of Israel. As you go, preach this message: The kingdom of heaven is near. Heal the sick, raise the dead, cleanse those who have leprosy, drive out demons (Matthew 10:5-8).

He knew Teddy would do much greater work among his own people. He sent Teddy back to tell the people what God had done for him. He knew this was no easy assignment because the town folks and cities were afraid of the former Teddy. They didn't even want to look at him, let alone listen to him. Jesus knew Teddy was strong and committed. He knew He had a true witness/evangelist/disciple/missionary and would give the newly revealed calling on his life all he had.

"This man became one of the earliest missionaries to the Gentiles. Jesus had to leave, but the man remained and bore faithful witness to the grace and power of Jesus Christ."[52] It wasn't long before all of Decapolis, Galilee, Judea, Jerusalem, and beyond Jordan flocked to hear and be healed by this caring and compassionate Savior.

And he departed and began to proclaim in **Decapolis** all that Jesus had done for him; and all marveled (Mark 5:20).

Then His fame went throughout all Syria; and they brought to Him all sick people who were afflicted with various diseases and torments, and those who were demon-possessed, epileptics, and paralytics; and He healed them. Great multitudes followed Him—from Galilee, and from **Decapolis**, Jerusalem, Judea, and beyond the Jordan (Matthew 4:24-25).

---

52. Warren Wiersbe, *Bible Exposition Commentary*, Vol. 1 (United States: Victor Books, 2003), 126.

Decapolis alone is approximately 1,200 square miles and comprises 10 cities. Who better to evangelize it than our boy Teddy? All Teddy had to say was, "Look at me. I'm the man you chained up in the tombs and forgot about. But Jesus didn't. He went out of His way to find me, for I once was lost but now am found. He gave me my life back and for that I will be forever grateful."

This story depicts the love two men had for each other. It beautifully portrays one wretched lost soul meeting and embracing Jesus Christ, God's Son the Savior.

Chapter Nine

Sibling Unrivalry: Martha, Mary, and Lazarus

This is a love story between three siblings—Martha, Mary, and Lazarus. Although opposites in some ways, together they conquered many pitfalls, always with Christ at the center. Be prepared to see the unusual. It is not the norm for brothers and sisters to coincide so harmoniously. When Martha and Mary saw that they were both righteous in their service to the Lord, they accepted each other's differences and relied on the Resurrection and the Life to lovingly spur them forward.

Let's start with a little background. All of the gospels mention various aspects of their lives, which took place in Bethany. Bethany is two miles southeast of Jerusalem, on the slope of the Mount of Olives. *Bethany* means "house of affliction, house of dates or figs." In other words, "Out of affliction comes fruit." It's almost as if the town was named just for this family. They certainly had their share of hardships.

Their father, Simon, had contracted leprosy, today known as Hansen's disease. This is an infection caused by a very specific, slow-spreading bacteria known as *Mycobacterium leprae*. It can be passed by means of nasal or oral emissions such as sneezing or coughing. Although contagious, it is not a super spreader because more than 95 percent of those infected fight it off with a healthy immune system. However, it is a much bigger problem in other parts of the world, mainly India. There is no vaccine for it.

We know Simon was the father because he was the owner of the house where the anointing took place.

> And when Jesus was in Bethany at the house of Simon the leper, a woman came to Him having an alabaster flask of very costly fragrant oil, and she poured it on His head as He sat at the table (Matthew 26:6-7).

We also know it to be the same house of Martha, Mary, and Lazarus. This town was the home of Jesus' friends Lazarus, Mary, and Martha, who were also present at this dinner. The woman who anointed Jesus' feet was Mary, Lazarus' and Martha's sister.[53]

Nothing is definitively known about Simon or his wife, who is never mentioned. We can learn more about them because of who their children were. By the time we meet Martha, Mary, and Lazarus they are already adults welcoming Jesus into their home. Whatever Simon did for a living, he left a rich legacy of prosperity and religious freedom. Jesus was so comfortable here He often stayed with the family whom he openly loved. This was a good place to teach His disciples and other guests. Unless Jesus departed to the mountain to be alone, He was always bombarded with questions, which led to great lessons and life-long commitments.

> Now Jesus loved Martha, and her sister, and Lazarus (John 11:5).

53. Footnote from Mark 14:3, *New King James Version: Life Application Study Bible* (United States: Tyndale House Publishers, Incorporated, 1996), 1795.

Losing their parents by their 30s, which is my best guess, may have been their biggest hardship thus far. Leprosy, at full throttle, affects three main areas: skin, nerves, and mucous membranes.

Symptoms and/or complications can include severe disfiguring, growths, numbness, blindness, hair loss, infertility, kidney failure, muscle weakness, nose bleeds, paralysis, and the list grows. Loss of limbs is often a result of injury or gangrene. It is curable if caught early and can be treated with antibiotics. If not caught early enough, it can lead to death. Once having received leprosy, the stigma never leaves. Why am I spending so much time on this? This is what Martha, Mary, and Lazarus had to deal with concerning their dad. They watched and waited day in and day out until their father was either taken away or died. I can only imagine what it must have been like for their mother.

Some years ago I went to Hawaii and island-hopped all over the place. There is a little island in the medley of Hawaiian islands called Molokai. Just off the Kalaupapa peninsula on Molokai is a leper colony founded 155 years ago. "In an effort to stop the spread of Hansen's disease, the Kingdom of Hawaii passed 'An Act to Prevent the Spread of Leprosy' in 1865, and designated Kalaupapa as the place where those with leprosy—and those suspected of having it—would reside. Hawaii purchased 800 acres of land on the Kalaupapa peninsula, surrounded by 2,000-foot cliffs, and began forcing people, mainly native Hawaiians, to Kalaupapa to live out the rest of their days, relying on themselves for food and resources. In January 1866, 12 Hawaiian citizens arrived at Kalaupapa, the first of about 8,000 people who were taken from their families and homes, and forced into isolation."[54]

I took an excursion and hopped aboard a prop plane and darn near went over a cliff on a donkey but finally arrived. Then we were loaded on a small tour bus. We went all around the old deserted town filled with

---

54. "Hawaii's Last Leprosy Community", Amanda Ogle, SFGATE, last modified May 11, 2021, https://www.sfgate.com/hawaii/article/2021-04-Hawaii-Molokai-Kalaupapa-leprosy-community-16143234.php.

ruins of the original leprosy colony. Before we disembarked at the car pick-up lot that would return us to the tiny airport, the tour guide spent a few minutes with us. He explained nobody came out because they are all ashamed. I asked, "What can we do for them?" He answered, "Don't come back. They're not objects of scorn on display. They're simple people like you and me. They want to live out their days peacefully and quietly." I was so convicted because I realized he was absolutely correct. I wanted to see the weird, the deformed, the ugly. All of these unfortunate folk are God's people, people for whom Jesus was crucified. Shame on me.

There are still a minimal number of patients there (6 to 16) between 73 and 92 years old. They lived a horrible life in a beautiful place. Their suffering is unimaginable. They were completely on their own. The colonies are now called quarantine communities. According to the World Health Organization there are approximately 208,000 infected with leprosy today throughout the world. Today there are many organizations that allow you to contribute to their leprosy community needs. I contribute to American Leprosy Missions in Greenville, South Carolina (www.leprosy.org).

Let's separate Martha, Mary, and Lazarus in order to reconnect them with the love they steadfastly had for one another despite their differences in character, never forgetting Jesus was at the center. Martha will go first. I believe she was the oldest because she took charge. She was bold and pragmatic. She knew what to do and was usually the first to get it done. She may have been a bit hyperaware. My daughter is that way. She is so aware of her environment that she knows before anyone else if someone is coming down the driveway, if a package has been delivered, or even if it starts raining. *Martha* means "dominant one, mistress, the feminine form of lord, master." Clearly, she is a take-charge kind of person. It's built in her DNA—she can't help but be who she is. Is she teachable? That remains to be seen. This doesn't make her bad or even wrong, but sometimes there is a better way.

Unfortunately, this story is best known for Martha doing all the work while her sister Mary sat at the feet of Jesus when He taught. Well, of course, after the teaching there would be no dinner prepared. You can't send the Master and His disciples away with no supper. Can you? Put yourself in her place.

> Now it came to pass, as they went, that he entered into a certain village: and a certain woman named Martha received him into her house. And she had a sister called Mary, which also sat at Jesus' feet, and heard his word. But Martha was cumbered about much serving, and came to him, and said, Lord, dost thou not care that my sister hath left me to serve alone? Bid her therefore that she help me. And Jesus answered and said unto her, Martha, Martha, thou are careful and troubled about many things (Luke 10:38-41).

So I did just that. Imagine Jesus coming to your house with very little notice as communication was limited at that time. What would your priorities be—get everything ready so Jesus, et al, would be impressed and sated or make ready as best you could until church started? Just knowing food was simmering and prepped would make them look forward all the more to its tasty arrival once the teaching concluded. We mustn't be too hard on Martha. It's easy to say, "If Jesus were in my house, everything can wait," but isn't He in your house, your heart, right now? How much time do you spend with Him? Jesus told Martha only one thing was needed—Him. What is the one "thing needful"? To come to Christ for salvation of the soul.[55]

> But one thing is needful: and Mary hath chosen that good part, which shall not be taken away from her (Luke 10:42).

---

55. William Smith, *Smith's Bible Dictionary Complete Concordance Revised Ed.* (Nashville, TN: Holman Bible Publishers, 1991), 421.

Mary is a beautiful example of someone who knew and valued what was most important. How did she get to this place in her young life? Let us remember who her father was—*Simon* in the Greek means "hearkening, hearing, hearing with acceptance, *hears and obeys*, an obeyer." Does that mean every Simon who heard the Word taught became a believer? Of course not, but can't we take a little latitude in that all three of his children not only believed but called Jesus Lord? In addition, not only did she suffer the death of her parents but then watched, horrified as her brother got sicker and sicker. No, this wasn't happening. Bad enough once, but twice? Were they cursed? Why them? Why him? Where was Jesus?

Mary, another name for *Miriam,* means "bitterness; rebellion; obstinate." The root of this name means "trouble; sorrow; disobedience." The Greek version means "sparkling light; star of the sea; celebrated." Whew! Just think of all the wonderful Marys in the good book as well as the Marys you may know personally. My beloved maternal grandmother is a good example. For Mary of Bethany, life must have been an uphill battle. But why? Except for some passive aggressive behavior such as not helping Martha as much as she could or not running with her sister to meet Jesus once He finally arrived, I see no transgressions. Do you?

> Then Martha, as soon as she heard that Jesus was coming, went and met him: but Mary sat still in the house (John 11:20).

We know Mary loved Jesus deeply. Earlier in His ministry, He taught a parable to the Pharisees regarding a similar occasion of being anointed by a woman with an alabaster box filled with precious ointment, which we will soon see in this story. The parable taught that those who sin the most, when forgiven, love the most. Mary will remain a bit of a mystery because of her elusive past. Maybe there is more here than meets the eye. Scripture does not reveal the siblings' background, but we can look at Mary and see a deep hunger and thirst for the Living Word. She knew when she was in the presence of greatness. She was very comfortable at His feet. Here she could fill her soul with Living Water from the well of salvation. This allowed her to live a life of righteousness, honoring God with every thought, word, and deed. Let that be our story. Let our legacy be one of seeking the Lord with all our heart and soul. Let us hunger for the true and living God making every day count with a fresh anointing.

> With joy you will draw water from the wells of salvation (Isaiah 12:3).

Lazarus means "God has ruled; without help." The Greek version *Eleazar* means "whom God helps or aids; the help of God; God is helper." Isn't it interesting that some of these meanings are prophetic to what became of them versus what they would become? I believe Lazarus was the youngest of the three. We first meet him in John 11:1. He is introduced as sick, so sick that the sisters are calling for Jesus. In response to their call, Jesus said something very interesting to his disciples. "This sickness is not unto death." Naturally they responded in kind and more or less dismissed Jesus' additional words, "but for the glory of God."

> Now a certain man was sick, named Lazarus, of Bethany, the town of Mary and her sister Martha. Therefore his sisters sent unto him, saying, Lord, behold, he whom thou lovest is sick. When Jesus heard that, He said, This sickness is not unto death, but for the glory of God, that the Son of God might be glorified thereby (John 11:1, 3-4).

It is believed that Lazarus had sepsis, a progressive illness starting with some kind of infection working its way into his bloodstream resulting in septic shock. According to Dr. William Lynes, "Being a physician, I may sometimes look at the Bible in a clinical manner. The story of Lazarus shows documented awesome power of the man from Galilee, Jesus Christ."[56]

At the time of Martha and Mary's petition, Jesus and His students were two days away, north along the Jordan River. Then Jesus did another surprising thing. He stayed another two days! Shockingly, He was in no rush to save His friend's life.

> Now Jesus loved Martha and her sister and Lazarus. So, when He heard that he was sick, He stayed two more days in the place where He was. Then after this He said to the disciples, "Let us go to Judea again." The disciples said to Him, "Rabbi, lately the Jews sought to stone You, and are You going there again?" (John 11:5-8)

It wasn't until He announced they were going to Judea that the disciples tried to dissuade Him, and for good reason. In the recent past while speaking in the temple on two separate occasions, the Pharisees picked up stones with the intent of stoning Jesus for what they perceived was blasphemy.

> Jesus said to them, "Most assuredly, I say to you, before Abraham was, I AM." Then they took up stones to throw at Him; but Jesus hid Himself and went out of the temple, going through the midst of them, and so passed by (John 8:58-59).

> "I and My Father are one." Then the Jews took up stones again to stone Him (John 10:30-31).

As the disciples continued to press Jesus, He revealed this outcome was prophesied 800 years prior by Isaiah.

---

56. "Lazarus Forensic Pathology of the Bible," William Lynes, last modified March 22, 2021, https://www.lynesonline.com.

The people who walked in darkness have seen a great light; Those who dwelt in the land of the shadow of death, Upon them a light has shined (Isaiah 9:2).

The very statements Jesus used to open the minds of the Pharisees, such as, "I am the light of the world," and "He who follows Me shall not walk in darkness," are the reasons they concluded He was a blasphemer (John 8:12).

Jesus was reminding His disciples that He must go while it is day—while He was still with them. He must go to reveal this great truth so they could see who He *really* was. They needed to witness that He is the Light of the world. John 9:5)

Sadly for them, seeing was believing. Thomas spoke for all of them when he said, "Let's go so we can die with Him" (John 11:16). He didn't mean Lazarus; he meant Jesus. Was this a noble or cynical remark? Either way it showed his ignorance. Jesus had to say to him later, "Seeing you believed, blessed are those who don't see but believe" (John 20:29). I take that to mean you and me.

Then Jesus arrived. Now we come to the great event that caused many to believe. He first saw Martha and told her point blank that Lazarus would rise again because He is the Resurrection and the Life. Yet she, too, did not believe or even get what He was saying to her. She knew Jesus was close to God but not necessarily God Himself. As the Son, she thought, He had to get permission like any other son. God the Father would give whatever His Son would ask. Martha was still not connecting the dots.

> Jesus said to her, "Your brother will rise again." Martha said to Him, "I know he will rise again in the resurrection at the last day." Jesus said to her, "I am the resurrection and the life. He who believes in Me, though he may die, he shall live. And whoever lives and believes in Me shall

never die. Do you believe this?" She said to Him, "Yes, Lord, I believe that You are the Christ, the Son of God, who is to come into the world" (John 11:23-27).

Then He presented her with an enigma. "If you die believing I am the resurrection and the life, you'll live. If you live and believe in Me you shall never die. Either way you live eternally." You and I will not taste of spiritual death. Hallelujah! Jesus explains a little further into His ministry that soon the world will no longer see Him, but He would not leave us orphans. He would replace Himself with the Spirit of Truth to live within us.

> If you love Me, you will keep My commandments. And I will pray the Father, and He will give you another Helper, that He may abide with you forever—the Spirit of Truth, whom the world cannot receive, because it neither sees Him nor knows Him; but you know Him, for He dwells with you and will be in you (John 14:15-17).

Then Mary came, weeping. Her words, similar to Martha's, expressed belief in Him as Lord and Healer but not the Resurrection and the Life. When He saw everyone weeping, He was so moved in His spirit with compassion that He also wept. He fully sensed their sadness. Have you ever thought of God that way? It seems easy to think of Him as *All Powerful, All Knowing, All Present, Creator, Conqueror*, but God who cries, God who can be sad and sorrowful, God who can be sad over our sadness? Yes, Jesus cried.

Jesus wept (John 11:35).

While the shortest verse in the Bible, it is the most poignant. It shows God's heart—how He loves us. He feels what we feel. He doesn't want us sad, depressed, lonely, longing, or grieving. There are no tears in heaven for a reason.

> He is despised and rejected by men, A man of sorrows
> and acquainted with grief (Isaiah 53:3a).

> For we have not a high priest which cannot be touched with
> the feeling of our own infirmities (Hebrews 4:15a KJV).

The utter depth of Jesus' frustration is what I believe caused Him to groan/sigh in His spirit. Over three years of ministry, teaching, and healing had passed, yet the most important and amazing thing about Him had yet to be grasped—He was God the Son, the Resurrection and the Life. As yet, no one really knew Him as God's Son and His time was running out. They merely related to His humanity as a healer, prophet, minister. They didn't know that God is plural, three Persons in One, the Father, Son, and Holy Spirit.

You are not you without your spirit and soul. They didn't know that the Son not only could give life but that it was *His desire* to give life. He was sent for that reason, and with that He commanded they roll the stone away covering the mouth of Lazarus' tomb and cried loudly for Lazarus to come out. Suddenly, there he stood alive and well wrapped in grave clothes, a glorious testimony to the Resurrection and the Life, "clothed with humanity,"[57] who also stood there smiling, ready to greet him back from the dead. Except for being hungry, Lazarus came back to life from irreversible death without the normal attributes of a decomposed corpse—ice cold, pale, rigor mortis, blue lips and finger nails, not to mention a horrible stench exacerbated by the Mediterranean climate.

> Then they took away the stone from the place where the
> dead man was lying. And Jesus lifted up his eyes and
> said, "Father, I thank You that You have heard Me. And I
> know that You always hear Me, but because of the people

---

57. "What does it mean that Jesus is the Firstborn Over Creation," Got Questions Ministries, accessed July 8, 2022, https://www.gotquestions.org/Jesus-first-born.html.

who are standing by I said this, that they may believe that
You sent Me (John 11:41-44).

The story could probably end nicely here were it not for one more
significant event that took place at the siblings' house. Just before the
last supper, Jesus dined one last time in Bethany with His three friends.
A great crowd came to see Jesus and Lazarus out of morbid curiosity.
Martha served, but this time without complaint. Martha learned through
Jesus' patience and love for her family that acceptance was the only way.
Albeit three individuals who were so different—Martha the busy one,
Mary the spiritually hungry one, and Lazarus the quiet one. It wasn't her
desire to serve that changed, it was serving with joy, serving from the
heart that changed. I believe if she had to climb the Mount of Olives to
gather figs, she would have done it gladly. There was no more bitterness
or frustration. She reconciled to "the better part" because she found out
that her friend Jesus was Jesus the Christ, Jesus the Messiah, God the
Son in the flesh, as did her whole family. She knew He loved her for
who she was. After all, He made her that way. He made her sister and
brother the way they were. Yet He loved them all the same. What could
be better than that?

All four gospels assume one lodging at Bethany during the last
week. One town, one house, one anointing. After dinner, Mary went
straight up to Jesus while He reclined at the table and broke the tip of an
alabaster flask of exquisite perfume and began pouring it over His head.
Then she wiped off His feet with her hair.

> Then, six days before the Passover, Jesus came to Beth-
> any, where Lazarus was who had been dead, whom He
> had raised from the dead. There they made Him a supper;
> and Martha served, but Lazarus was one of those who sat
> at the table with Him. Then Mary took a pound of very
> costly oil of spikenard, anointed the feet of Jesus, and

wiped His feet with her hair. And the house was filled
with the fragrance of the oil (John 12:1-3).

Alabaster flasks were carved from a translucent gypsum. These jars
were used to hold perfumed oil.[58] An alabaster flask was a beautiful and
expensive carved vase. Oil of spikenard was expensive perfume.[59] She
had the passion to do this, but probably had no idea why she did it, at
least not until Jesus explained to the practical minded disciples its significance. Have you ever felt prompted to do something that wasn't part
of your plan? Maybe suddenly write or call someone you hadn't spoken
to in a long time, or buy a gift and secretly deliver it to someone? How
about just start praying for someone fervently? Sure you have. That's
God's Spirit moving on your spirit to act on your faith. That's the kind
of altruistic work that will count when measured in heaven.

> According to the grace of God which is given unto me, as a
> wise master builder, I have laid the foundation, and another
> buildeth thereon. But let every man take heed how he buil-
> deth thereupon. For other foundation can no man lay than
> that is laid, which is Jesus Christ. Now if any man build
> upon this foundation gold, silver, precious stones, wood,
> hay, stubble; Every man's work shall be made manifest: for
> the day shall declare it, because it shall be revealed by fire;
> and the fire shall try every man's work of what sort it is. If
> any man's work abide which he hath built thereupon, he
> shall receive a reward (1 Corinthians 3:10-14).

Mary's action was no small matter. Jesus was praising Mary for
her unselfish act of worship. The essence of worshiping Christ is to
regard Him with utmost love, respect, and devotion and to be willing to

---

58. Footnote from Matthew 26:7B, *New King James Version: Life Application Study Bible*
(United States: Tyndale House Publishers, Incorporated, 1996), 1736.

59.Footnote from Mark 14:3, *New King James Version: Life Application Study Bible* (United
States: Tyndale House Publishers, Incorporated, 1996), 1795.

sacrifice to Him what is most precious.[60] The Lord used Mary to prepare everyone present—family, friends, disciples, Pharisees—for His crucifixion. What an honor! Pouring sweet, scented oil, her most precious possession, over her Lord and Master's head, then wiping His feet with her hair in front of all present after the precious oil covered His body took *chutzpah,* which means "quality of audacity for good or for bad." Deep inside, she knew somehow this was what she was supposed to do for their long-term honored guest. Interestingly, the disciples, specifically Judas Iscariot, grumbled about Mary's very generous gesture. It wasn't even his to priggishly criticize how it could have been better used. (Notice, not a peep out of Martha.) Jesus quickly corrected them and revealed this act was both prophetic and symbolic of His crucifixion and burial because soon He would no longer be among them.

> But Jesus said, "Let her alone; she has kept this for the day of My burial. For the poor you have with you always, but Me you do not have always" (John 12:7-8).

Lazarus, who had been sitting there, didn't have to say or do anything. He was chosen to reveal to the world that Jesus was the Resurrection and the Life. He had already fulfilled the most important role of his life—being a type of Christ. There was a cost to this honorable role—it put a target on his head. It wasn't enough that the chief priests knew he had already once suffered and died, but they schemed his demise again just because many Jews went away believing all the more in their nemesis—Jesus Christ. Lazarus was now a part of Jesus' story. The chief priests wanted Lazarus dead simply because he was a living witness to Jesus' power.[61] God's plan was working. To consult to hinder the further effect of the miracle by putting Lazarus to death is such wickedness, malice, and folly, as cannot be explained, except by the desperate enmity

---

60. Footnote from Mark 14:6-7, *New King James Version: Life Application Study Bible* (United States: Tyndale House Publishers, Incorporated, 1996), 1796.
61. Footnote from John 12:10-11, *New King James Version: Life Application Study Bible* (United States: Tyndale House Publishers, Incorporated, 1996), 1932.

of the human heart against God. They resolved that the man should die whom the Lord had raised to life. The success of the gospel often makes wicked men so angry that they speak and act as if they hoped to obtain a victory over the Almighty Himself.[62]

> But the chief priests plotted to put Lazarus to death also, because on account of him many of the Jews went away and believed in Jesus (John 12:10-11).

We know that one of Jesus' disciples aided and abetted the chief priests—Judas. He is the only person in all of humanity's history to unequivocally be recorded as the son of perdition who went to hell. Imagine having on your life's report card an F for betraying God, the Creator of the universe.

How was Lazarus a type of Christ? He was dead four days and went out quietly. Jesus was dead three days and went out silent as a lamb led to the slaughter. As we have already seen, Lazarus was a victim of a deadly infection, which led to his demise. Jesus was also a victim of a deadly disease known as the sinful pride of others. Satan, the brain-child of this atrocity, was consumed with pride (and still is), which he passed on to the Jewish leaders. The chief priests were jealous and fearful they would lose their following. They also feared that Rome would take away their status. So, they purposed to remove Jesus from the face of the earth and send Him to the grave or tomb. Lazarus was raised from the dead, having lived in captivity with the righteous saints waiting for their promised Deliverer. Jesus, the Son of heaven Himself, died and rose again taking captivity captive to heaven above. "He conquered those who had conquered us; such as sin, the devil, and death."[63]

---

62. Matthew Henry, *Concise Commentary on the Whole Bible* (Chicago: Moody Press, 1983), 792.

63. Matthew Henry, *The Amplified Bible*, Footnote from Ephesians 4:8, (Grand Rapids, MI: Zondervan Bible Publishers, 1984), 299.

You have ascended on high. You have led away captive a train of vanquished foes; You have received gifts of men, yes, of the rebellious also, that the Lord God might dwell there with them (Psalm 68:18).

Yet grace (God's unmerited favor) was given to each of us individually [not indiscriminately, but in different ways] in proportion to the measure of Christ's [rich and bounteous] gift. Therefore it is said, When He ascended on high, He led captivity captive [He led a train of vanquished foes] and He bestowed gifts on men (Ephesians 4:7-8 AMPC).

Martha, with her gift of hospitality, kept them coming so that believing and unbelieving Jews were gathered in one place. Mary's role was to unite the believers and cause them to make ready in their hearts for what was soon to come. In order to know that Jesus was really God, they had to know God could not permanently die, unlike so many heroes from the past or the gods of false religions. Jesus raising Lazarus was just another incredible thing He did for us. In order to fully experience the "better part" Jesus had to demonstrate within His own power that not only could He raise man, He could also, as part of the Triune Godhead, raise Himself.

Jesus answered and said unto them, Destroy this temple, and in three days I will raise it up (John 2:19).

Additionally, John the Baptist, by Jesus' own words, was a messenger whose job was to prepare the way a little more than six months ahead of Jesus. He baptized with water, the baptism of repentance. Jesus would come baptizing with the Holy Spirit and with fire.

For this is He, of whom it is written, Behold, I send my messenger before thy face, which shall prepare thy way before thee (Matthew 11:10).

Lazarus laid the path a little more than six days ahead of Jesus. He left this world only to be raised again by Jesus, the Son. In a sense they were both God-appointed messengers. John the Baptist's mission in life was to announce the coming of the Savior. Lazarus' destiny in life was to announce, by proxy, the death, burial, and resurrection of the Savior—Jesus Christ. God has given each of us a purpose for living. And we can trust Him to guide us. God can use you in a way He can use no one else.[64]

We hear no more about Martha, Mary, and Lazarus. We don't know where they were when Jesus was crucified, entombed, and resurrected. I believe during that dark time in history they were together and at peace deep in their hearts knowing what the outcome would be. They witnessed the preview; they played a big part in the trailer to the greatest story ever told. Their Lord and Master chose their town, Bethany, from which to rise and join His Father in order to at last reap the fruit of His affliction.

> And He led them out as far as Bethany, and He lifted up His hands and blessed them. Now it came to pass, while He blessed them, that He was parted from them and carried up into heaven (Luke 24:50-51).

Their fervent love for one another, with Christ at the center, the One thing needed, solidified and sustained them until the next time they would all be together again—in eternity.

---

64. Insert of John the Baptist, *New King James Version: Life Application Study Bible* (United States: Tyndale House Publishers, Incorporated, 1996), 1899.

Chapter Ten

God Come in the Flesh: Jesus Messiah

As God knew us before the foundation of the world, He knew our imperfection would require a plan to bring us to Himself. Hence the garden, the choice to obey or not, the plan of redemption, the unfolding. God is love and no unrighteousness can be found in Him. He is, was, and always will be perfect. He is the perfection of beauty. He is what every man and woman should strive to become during their short stay on earth. He can be trusted.

Throughout the Old Testament, prophets, stories, examples, promises, types, and shadows illustrated the plan culminating in Messiah's arrival in the form of human likeness.

> But when the proper time had fully come, God sent His Son, born of a woman, born subject to the law (Galatians 4:4 AMPC).

> Let this same attitude and purpose and mind be in you which was in Christ Jesus. [Let Him be your example in humility:] Who, although being essentially one with God and in the form of God, did not think this equality with

179

God was a thing to be eagerly grasped or retained, But stripped Himself [of all privileges and rightful dignity] so as to assume the guise of a servant, in that He became like men and was born a human being. And after He had appeared in human form He abased and humbled Himself and carried His obedience to the extreme of death, even the death of the cross! (Philippians 2:5-8 AMPC)

The Holy Spirit of God came upon the virgin, Mary, as foretold to both her and her betrothed (promised) husband-to-be, Joseph. Jesus always referred to His heavenly Father when teaching, praying, or worshiping. Since God is One, *Elohim* in Hebrew, I take this to mean God the Father *and* God the Holy Spirit, the first and third members of the triune Godhead. Finally, at the perfect apex in time, our Savior was born.

Therefore the Lord Himself shall give you a sign; Behold, a virgin shall conceive, and bear a son, and shall call his name Immanuel [God is with us] (Isaiah 7:14 AMPC).

Now the birth of Jesus Christ took place under these circumstances: When His mother Mary had been promised in marriage to Joseph, before they came together she was found to be pregnant [through the power] of the Holy Spirit. But as he (Joseph) was thinking this over, behold, an angel of the Lord appeared to him in a dream, saying, Joseph, descendant of David, do not be afraid to take Mary [as] your wife, for that which is conceived in her is of (from, out of) the Holy Spirit (Matthew 1:18, 20 AMPC).

And the angel answered and said to her [Mary], "The Holy Spirit will come upon you, and the power of the Highest will overshadow you; therefore...[the child] to be born will be called Holy, the Son of God (Luke 1:35 AMPC).

"The word 'therefore' in Luke 1:35 is tremendously important. It shows that the conception of Jesus in a virgin is owing to the mysterious work of the Holy Spirit. And it shows that the divine Sonship of Jesus depends on His virgin birth.... Jesus can be called the Son of God, Son of the Most High, precisely because He was 'conceived by the Holy Spirit, born of the virgin Mary.' " Through Him, the Father caused the Son to be conceived. The conception of Jesus is owing to the mysterious work of the Holy Spirit. Jesus is uniquely God's Son, the divine Word and image of God, begotten from all eternity.[65]

God the Father and the Holy Spirit cannot be separated. It is dangerous to try and separate God—Elohim. Without three members, God is not complete. You can no more separate your soul from your spirit. Once they leave the body, you are declared dead. Even when the Word became flesh, Jesus was still considered the Son of God/God the Son. Any religion that deems one member only to be God is a false religion.

> In the beginning was the Word, and the Word was with
> God, and the Word was God. He was in the beginning with
> God. And the Word was made flesh, and dwelt among us,
> (and we beheld His glory, the glory as of the only begotten
> of the Father,) full of grace and truth (John 1:1-2, 14 KJV).

Many cultures throughout history believed that gods, as immortal beings, could not bleed. However, God's Son, Jesus, became human so that His blood would be shed for a new covenant. Truly this was God in the flesh.

> Gather My saints together to Me, Those who have made
> a covenant with Me by sacrifice (Psalm 50:5).

---

65. "Christ Conceived by the Holy Spirit," John Piper, DesiringGod.com, accessed July 9, 2022, https://www.desiringgod.org/messages/christ-conceived-by-the-holy-spirit.

The Holy Spirit was upon Him throughout His 33 1/2 years incarnate. When Jesus left the earth, the Holy Spirit was sent back to teach, anoint, remind us of all things, and comfort us. We have the same access to Him as Jesus did. If we are in Christ, we too, are sons and daughters of the living Elohim and can be indwelt and infilled with the Holy Spirit.

> The Spirit of the Lord is upon Me, because He hath anointed Me to preach the gospel to the poor; He hath sent me to heal the brokenhearted, to preach deliverance to the captives, and recovering of sight to the blind, to set at liberty them that are bruised (Luke 4:18 KJV).

> Now when the apostles who were at Jerusalem heard that Samaria had received the word of God, they sent Peter and John to them, who, when they had come down, prayed for them that they might receive the Holy Spirit. For as yet He had fallen upon none of them. They had only been baptized in the name of the Lord Jesus. Then they laid hands on them and they received the Holy Spirit (Acts 8:14-17).

He left the glory of kingship to become a lowly, often rejected, and very misunderstood young man. And so the journey begins. Except for the heavenly birth, by all appearances, Jesus was no different than any other man, flesh and blood—God in the flesh. He was born of Jewish descent, because as part of the plan God chose Israel, a tiny country in the middle of the map, to reveal Himself to the rest of the world. Surrounded by enemies all around, He has safeguarded them over the past 4,200 years making them a great nation on May 14, 1948. Starting with the lineage of Adam, the loyalty of Enoch, the dedication of Noah, the faith of Abraham, the valor of David, and ending with the humility of Jesus. Against all odds, God has raised up a resilient people, far from perfect, but unique. Within this godly heritage are Essenes, scribes, and Jewish historians eager to preserve the history and oracles of God. Yes, the Jews have been dealt with severely, scattered and brought back over and over again. *Aliyah*, the returning of Jews from all over the world back to Israel, is happening even as I write these words.

Nations such as Assyria, Babylon, and Germany committed mass murder against them; terrorists such as Hamas and Hezbollah are backed by Iran, who is backed by Russia in an effort to wipe them off the face of the earth. Transient people from Trans Jordan and surrounding areas have settled there such as the self-proclaimed "Palestinians" who despise them and want to see them gone. That's why religious wars are so dangerous. One or both sides believe they are fighting for the cause of their god. These so-called holy wars can go on for decades, sometimes centuries. What motivates these religious fanatics is the belief they will be regarded with some kind of eternal recognition and pleasure they can't get in this life. One thing these religious sects all have in common is their distrust and unyielding jealousy over Jesus. The common denominator behind every attempt to annihilate the people God chose to reveal Himself is the unseen major player—Satan, the dragon himself.

God has another plan. He gave to this precious charge the responsibility of leading all people to Him. He gave them the Commandments, the Law, the Prophets, His Son, and the responsibility of upholding a commission directly ordered by Christ, Yeshua Himself. Yes, the Jews are God's chosen people but they missed their window of opportunity. Weeping, Jesus said,

> For a time is coming upon you when your enemies will throw up a bank [with pointed stakes] about you and surround you and shut you in on every side. And they will dash you down to the ground, you [Jerusalem] and your children within you; and they will not leave in you one stone upon another, [all] because you did not come progressively to recognize and know and understand [from observation and experience] the time of your visitation

183

[that is, when God was visiting you, the time in which
God showed Himself gracious toward you and offered
you salvation through Christ] (Luke 19:43-44 AMPC).

God, in turn, gave this time to the Gentiles now known as the church
age. People from all nations, races, and tongues have learned of Christ.
This "age" will last until the "rapture" when the church will be taken
away. Then you will know you are in the end of the end times. Yes,
people will be saved, but it will be during a period of tribulation, a time
when identifying who you really are in Christ could be treacherous.

And they shall fall by the edge of the sword, and shall
be led away captive into all nations: and Jerusalem shall
be trodden down of the Gentiles, until the times of the
Gentiles be fulfilled (Luke 21:24).

Today there are Messianic Jews—Jewish people who recognize
Jesus as the true Messiah—who are doing an impressive job reaching
their non-believing brothers and sisters. There are many organizations
that support this cause. Two that stand out are:

1) The International Fellowship of Christians and Jews. They not only
   provide Aliyah (fly Jews into Israel from all over the world) but
   support the elderly Holocaust survivors still existing in freezing
   cold, isolated places such as Siberia.[66]

2) Keren Ahvah Meshihit—Messianic Brotherhood Fund.[67]

Forty years ago I visited their warehouse in Jerusalem where Bibles
and books were published in Hebrew and distributed for evangelism
throughout Israel. In both cases, the children of the deceased fathers
that founded these ministries are continuing to fulfill their dreams to

---

66. PO Box 97339, Washington DC, 20077-7472, www.ifcj.org.
67. 15 Lankin Eliahu, Jerusalem, Israel, 9339931 www.Kerenahvah.org.

reach and bless the Jewish people with the knowledge that Yeshua is Israel's Messiah.

Things aren't exactly smooth and easy right now. All the signs are in place. There are wars and rumors of wars. Terrorists are taking over where there is no more American or allied presence. There are earthquakes, famines, floods, and persecutions of horrific magnitude. We will get to the point where the world government will force mother to turn against child, father to turn against mother, children to turn against their parents and each other. Many will do this because they believe they are doing the right thing. Many will betray their neighbors motivated by greed and opportunity. Many will betray their loved ones from a deep sense of fear. And on it will go until the tribulation, worse than any other time period in human history, will serve as the war cry for God the Son to return and rescue what's left of His people—Jew and Gentile alike.

> For then there will be great tribulation (affliction, distress and oppression) such as has not been from the beginning of the world until now; no, and never will be [again] (Matthew 24:21 AMPC).

> He [the second beast or false prophet] was granted power to give breath to the image of the [first] beast, that the image of the beast should both speak and cause as many as would not worship the image of the beast to be killed. He causes all, both small and great, rich and poor, free and slave, to receive a mark on their right hand or on the foreheads, and that no one may buy or sell except one who has the mark or the name of the beast, or the number of his name (Revelation 13:15-17).

The year was A.D. 16-18. Hungry to serve, twelve-year-old Jesus sat with rabbis in the temple listening and contemplating arguments and debates concerning the Torah (the first five books of the Old Testament).

He answered questions as easily as an orchestral conductor brushes whole passages with a baton. Despite being God's Son, He submitted to His earthly parents' authority and went back with them to Nazareth because it was not yet His time, the time of Jewish priesthood. He emerged 18 years later, full of wisdom, maturity, and the Holy Spirit and was "moved from within" to the wilderness or desert to be tested.

> Then Jesus, full of and controlled by the Holy Spirit, returned from the Jordan, and was led in the Spirit for forty days in the wilderness [or desert], where He was tempted (tested exceedingly) by the devil (Luke 4:1-2a).

In the wilderness, humanity's archenemy, the former archangel Lucifer renamed Satan, challenged Jesus three times. These were in the areas of authority, pride, and commitment. Jesus went 40 days without food, and it is a real eye-opener in the spirit realm. (This must only be done as led of the Lord.) God inspired the authors of the Gospels to write what we "had a need to know." Therefore, it stands to reason the devil may have attempted to entice Jesus to defect from God in other ways as well. We do know Jesus knew who He was, why He was sent, and was utterly committed to His Father God and the Holy Spirit.

Jesus continued to grow and teach with authority and power but not without setbacks. When Jesus went on the road at 30 years of age, His dining consisted of kosher meals laden with questions to put Him on the defensive by Jewish leaders or questions to put Him in the role of educator to lessen the ignorance displayed by His disciples. He did not sleep on a comfortable bed with a mattress cover, sheets, and a quilt. Instead, there were flying and crawling bugs, spiders, and dangerous forest animals all about with only rocks and tree debris to rest His head. Warmth was gleaned from a fire, entertainment did not exist except in conversations with His men.

Ah, then there were His men. Often times they were afraid of Him. Just as often He told them not to be troubled or afraid. His message was so fantastic that He had to repeat and demonstrate it over and over knowing they were, as yet, in way over their head. They were typical, ordinary men with two things in common. First, they wanted to be a part of something big. Next, they knew their destiny lay in the hands of this magnificent Man who appeared tender and gentle yet powerful and determined. Jesus recognized their hunger to serve the living God.

> And they were astonished at His doctrine: for His word
> was with power (Luke 4:32).

Early on, emotional pain was inflicted. The first to reject Him was His own hometown, i.e. His closest friends, neighbors, relatives, and teachers of His own Word. It was one thing to be doubted and barraged with questions, but quite another to "heal only a few." The lack of faith in this section of Galilee led to fewer people witnessing and thereby believing in the works of the Healer, which could lead to their salvation.

> Then He went out from there and came to His own coun-
> try, and His disciples followed Him. And when the Sab-
> bath had come, he began to teach in the synagogue. And
> many hearing Him were astonished, saying, "Where did
> this Man get these things? And what wisdom is this which
> is given to Him, that such mighty works are performed
> by His hands! Is this not the carpenter, the Son of Mary,
> and brother of James, Joses, Judas, and Simon? And are
> not His sisters here with us?" So they were offended at
> Him (Mark 6:1-3).

> So they were offended at Him. But Jesus said to them, "A
> prophet is not without honor except in His own country
> and in His own house." Now He did not do many mighty
> works here because of their unbelief (Matthew 13:57-8).

Even at His first reading, many responded with jealous outrage. He went to His hometown synagogue in Nazareth as He usually did. He stood up and read from Isaiah.

> So He came to Nazareth, where He had been brought up. And as His custom was, He went into the synagogue on the Sabbath day, and stood up to read (Luke 4:16).

> The Spirit of the Lord [is] upon Me, because He has anointed Me [the Anointed One, the Messiah] to preach the good news (the Gospel) to the poor; He has sent Me to announce release to the captives and recovery of sight to the blind, to send forth as delivered those who are oppressed [who are downtrodden, bruised, crushed, and broken down by calamity] (Luke 4:18 AMPC).

> Then He closed the book, and gave it back to the attendant and sat down. And the eyes of all who were in the synagogue were fixed on Him. And He began to say to them, "Today this scripture is fulfilled in your hearing" (Luke 4:20-21).

> The Spirit of the Lord God is upon me, because the Lord has anointed and qualified me to preach the Gospel of good tidings to the meek, the poor and afflicted; He has sent me to bind up and heal the brokenhearted, to proclaim liberty to the captives and the opening of the prison and of the eyes to those who are bound (Isaiah 61:1).

He sat back down and explained how that scripture on that day was fulfilled. Knowing their hearts, He also said He knew His words were not accepted. He knew they wouldn't accept Him as a prophet either. Their doubt would be the reason He wouldn't be able to perform the same miracles He would administer in other places. For this reason they got angry and sought to shove Him over a cliff. (Have you ever gotten furious at someone and thought later how ridiculous that was or couldn't even remember how the fight started in the first place?) This, no doubt, would be a Via Dolorosa journey from Galilee all the way to the cross.

> And He said, Verily I say unto you, No prophet is accepted in his own country. And all they in the synagogue, when they heard these things, were filled with wrath, And rose up, and thrust Him out of the city, and led Him unto the brow of the hill whereon their city was built, that they might cast Him down headlong (Luke 4:24, 28-29 KJV).

Then, not too long after, His beloved cousin John was executed. How painful this must have been. He barely knew John in human form yet chose him before the foundation of the world. He created him.

> Blessed be the God and Father of our Lord Jesus Christ, who has blessed us with every spiritual blessing in the heavenly places in Christ, just as He chose us in Him before the foundation of the world, that we should be holy and without blame before Him in love (Ephesians 1:3-4).

> All things were made through Him, and without Him nothing was made that was made (John 1:3).

Scripture tells us that one of Jesus' coping methods was to minister to the multitudes when times got tough, such as He did once hearing of John the Baptist's beheading. This has really ministered to me. Whenever the devil attacks, I pray for that category of people all the more. For example, if I learn someone has just been diagnosed with leukemia, I pray for them, then everyone else suffering with that disease. If I experience flu-like symptoms, I pray for everyone with the flu. I use my spiritual weapons to fight spiritual warfare.

Two separate times are recorded when Jesus publicly wept. The first was when He saw mourners of Lazarus, brother of Martha and Mary, not yet believing He was the Resurrection and the Life. The second, which is where I want to focus, was shortly thereafter when Jesus was making His triumphal entry into Jerusalem on an unbroken colt of a donkey. This in and of itself is nothing short of a miracle. Breaking colts or foals of donkeys is a slow, tedious process. While training a horse is similar, a trainer must take baby steps and build trust before attempting to ride it. The usual time allotted is about one year.

When reaching the summit of the Mount of Olives, Jesus had a chance to look upon His beloved city. In His mind's eye, He saw the devastation that would take place 40 short years later. Jerusalem would be a city torn down with its temple and people flattened to the ground because, as with sin, the door had been opened to Satan to bring destruction upon themselves.

All during the rough times and pleasant times of Jesus' growing ministry, He was reminded of His impending death. It's like anticipating the funeral of a close loved one scheduled later in the week. It puts a blight on everything. In addition, knowing which followers would fall away or how they would meet with their demise held a sorrowful motif. It took strength and effort to be about the business of His heavenly Father and to not show the sadness He must have continuously felt in His heart. Nonetheless, Jesus continued to teach and heal the multitudes, encourage His disciples, and glorify God up to His final breath. Whereby God honored Him with the highest honor in all of existence, which He has chosen to share with us as an inheritance.

> The God of our Lord Jesus Christ, the Father of glory, may give to you the spirit of wisdom and revelation in the knowledge of Him, the eyes of your understanding being enlightened; that you may know what is the hope of His calling, what are the riches of the glory of His

190

inheritance in the saints, and what is the exceeding greatness of His power toward us who believe, according to
the working of His mighty power which He worked in
Christ when He raised Him from the dead and seated
Him at His right hand in the heavenly places, far above
all principality and power and might and dominion, and
every name that is named, not only in this age but also in
that which is to come (Ephesians 1:18-21).

Imagine an existence in which you lived for the moment but knew
every aspect of a person's life. You knew if they were sincere. You knew
their future sins. You knew the risks they were willing to take on your
behalf. You knew their heart. You knew their thoughts before they were
fully formed. This is God's everyday world.

Many may not realize that the man part of Jesus was subject to all
temptations, which meant He Himself had to do the things He taught.
He healed but was exposed to every viral and bacterial sickness and
disease He cleansed.

And Jesus went about all Galilee, teaching in their syn-
agogues, and preaching the gospel of the kingdom, and
healing all kinds of sickness and all kinds of disease
among the people (Matthew 4:23).

In addition to His message, remembering every aspect of His own
Word written during the course of close to 550 years before that time,
He had to know how to apply it in any given situation. He had to know
how to deliver it, the written Word, wherever the Holy Spirit sent Him.
He might be in Capernaum one day and Gadara the next, or Jericho then
to Bethany. He was never late and always prepared. I don't suppose He
had any special training in public speaking in heaven. He had to know
how to defend or utilize apologetics when seemingly misunderstood.

As regarding the Sabbath:

Now it happened that He went through the grain fields on the Sabbath; and as they went His disciples began to pluck the heads of the grain. And the Pharisees said to Him, "Look, why do they do what is not lawful on the Sabbath?" But he said to them, "Have you never read what David did when he was in need and hungry, he and those with him; how he went into the house of God in the days of Abiathar the High Priest, and ate the showbread, which is not lawful to eat except for the priests, and also gave some to those who were with him?" And He said to them, "The Sabbath was made for man, and not man for the Sabbath. Therefore the Son of Man is also Lord of the Sabbath" (Mark 2:23-28).

As regarding the resurrection:

Then came to him certain of the Sadducees, which they deny that there is any resurrection; and they asked him, Saying, Master, Moses wrote unto us, If any man's brother die, having a wife, and he die without children, that his brother should take his wife, and raise up seed unto his brother. There were therefore seven brethren: and the first took a wife, and died without children. And the second took her to wife, and he died childless. And the third took her; and in like manner the seven also: and they left no children, and died. Last of all the woman died also. Therefore in the resurrection whose wife of them is she? For seven had her to wife. And Jesus answering said unto them, The children of this world marry, and are given in marriage: But they which shall be accounted worthy to obtain that world, and the resurrection from the dead, neither marry nor are given in marriage: Neither can they die any more: for they are equal unto the angels; and are the children of God, being the children of the resurrection (Luke 20:27-36).

As regarding the law:

> The scribes and Pharisees brought a woman along who had been caught committing adultery; and making her stand there in full view of everybody, they said to Jesus, "Master, this woman was caught in the very act of committing adultery, and Moses has ordered us in the law to condemn women like this to death by stoning. What have you to say?" They asked Him this as a test, looking for something to use against Him. But Jesus bent down and started writing on the ground with his finger. As they persisted with their question, He looked up and said, "If there is one of you who has not sinned, let him be the first to throw a stone at her" (John 8:3-7).

> It is also written in your law, that the testimony of two men is true. I am one that bear witness of myself, and the Father that sent me beareth witness of Me (John 8:17-18 KJV).

Furthermore, he suffered persecution in multiple forms. He had to exercise great patience with His disciples while performing the easier task of calming the sea.

> And, behold, there arose a great tempest in the sea, insomuch that the ship was covered with the waves: but He was asleep. And his disciples came to Him, and awoke Him, saying, Lord, save us: we perish. And He saith unto them, Why are ye fearful, O ye of little faith? Then He arose, and rebuked the winds and the sea; and there was a great calm. But the men marveled, saying, What manner of Man is this, that even the winds and the sea obey Him! (Matthew 8:24-27)

He had to teach faith while simply walking on water.

And Peter answered Him and said, Lord, if it be Thou, bid me come unto Thee on the water. And He said, Come. And when Peter was come down out of the ship, he walked on the water, to go to Jesus. But when he saw the wind boisterous, he was afraid; and beginning to sink. He cried, saying, Lord, save me. And immediately Jesus stretched His hand, and caught him and said unto him, O thou of little faith, wherefore didst thou doubt? And when they were come into the ship, the wind ceased (Matthew 14:28-32 KJV).

He had the arduous task of warning His disciples about false teaching while reminding them of the more compassionate task of multiplying the fishes and loaves.

Then Jesus said unto them, Take heed and beware of the leaven of the Pharisees and of the Sadducees. Do you not yet understand, neither remember the five loaves of the five thousand, and how many baskets ye took up? Neither the seven loaves of the four thousand, and how many baskets ye took up? How is it that you do not understand that I spake it not unto you concerning the bread, that you should be aware of the leaven of the Pharisees and of the Sadducees? (Matthew 16:6, 9-11)

Accustomed to angelic worship in heaven, now He was poked and prodded at every turn by the so-called experts of the Torah (the first five books of the Old Testament). Pharisees and/or Sadducees challenged Him every day with an achievement test in Jewish history, Judaism, and eschatology. Meanwhile, He was preparing to lay down His life and save them and the rest of the world.

> For even the Son of Man came not to be ministered unto,
> but to minister, and to give His life a ransom for many
> (Mark 10:45).

Adding insult to injury, after numerous miracles and demonstrations of mercy and forgiveness, and teaching the main principles of love, humility, giving, patience, trusting in God, and being born again, the chief priests, elders, and teachers dared challenge Jesus' authority. They were extremely jealous and therefore hated Him because they feared Him. They never knew what response He would give and were always afraid of being outdone by Him. Generally, His answers were not literal. They were designed to make them think and to expose their true motive and disloyalty to the God they professed to follow. He knew no matter how simple the question, they were out to get Him. If they could prove Him inadequate or contrary to the law in any way they would ruin His credibility and subsequently His reputation. Instead, most teachers left amazed and incredulous. Conversely, when He asked them a question they were stymied.

> Now when He came into the temple, the chief priests
> and the elders of the people confronted Him as He
> was teaching, and said, "By what authority are You
> doing these things? And Who gave You this author-
> ity?" (Matthew 21:23)

> But Jesus perceived their wickedness, and said, Why
> tempt ye Me, ye hypocrites? When they had heard these
> words, they marveled, and left Him, and went their way.
> And no man was able to answer Him a word, neither
> durst any man from that day forth ask Him any more
> questions (Matthew 22:18, 22, 46 KJV).

> So they could not in the presence of the people take hold
> of anything He said to turn it against Him; but marveling

at His reply they were silent. And some of the scribes
replied, Teacher, you have spoken well and expertly [so
that there is no room for blame]. For they did not dare to
question Him further (Luke 20:26,39-40 AMPC).

However, Jesus' life on earth wasn't all sadness and suffering. I firmly believe He enjoyed the previous Passover festivals;
those times in Bethany spent with His friends, Martha, Mary, and
Lazarus; the multitudes coming, believing, and receiving Him; His
disciples learning and growing; and above all else time spent alone
with His heavenly Father. This is where He would get refreshed
and receive strength through the agape love ministered to Him from
His Father and His Father's Spirit in order to carry out His mission
here on earth.

Finally, the night arrived when Jesus would enjoy a final dinner
with His disciples. It was a bittersweet meal. It was the last Passover meal, only this time the angel of death was heading straight
for Jesus. Jesus watched as Satan entered Judas Iscariot. He antic-
ipated that moment for three or more years. Somehow anticipation
and reality are disconnected. One can always hope that the pending
storm won't occur. One can always hope their job doesn't get elim-
inated. One can always hope their loved one will pull through the
operation. When the moment arrives and the manifestation of your
hopes isn't realized exactly as you had imagined, the disappoint-
ment is just as painful. Jesus loved Judas, living and walking and
talking with him for all those years. Would Judas change his mind at
the last second and choose not to betray Him? Already knowing the
answer and where he would end up made it no less painful.

Then Satan entered Judas, surname Iscariot, who was
numbered among the twelve (Luke 22:3).

As dinner wrapped up, it was time to go and pray. It was time for the Lamb of God to meet the dragon known as Satan face to face once again. It was Satan's turn to throw his best shot. Satan's cruel and relentless revenge would layer punishment after punishment on God's innocent Son. Down through the centuries Elohim witnessed the kind of evil Satan was capable of, starting with the brutal murder of Able in the field by Cain, his older brother.

> And Cain talked with Abel his brother: and it came to pass, when they were in the field, that Cain rose up against Abel his brother, and slew him (Genesis 4:8).

Anything Satan could impose to perpetrate his maniacal revenge on God, his Creator, for removing him from heaven. This would include sickness, disease, abuse, torture to and by humans to other humans, animals, and nature. He thought higher of himself than he had any right to imagine let alone carry out one horrific act after another on God's people and His creation.

Look at what Satan inflicted upon Job, a decent, well-to-do man who loved God. Because of this, Satan sought God's permission to hurt him beyond what most men could bear in order to prove a point.

> Then the Lord said to Satan, "Have you considered My servant Job, that there is none like him on the earth, a blameless and upright man, one who fears God and shuns evil?" So Satan answered the Lord and said, "Does Job fear God for nothing? Have You not made a hedge around him, around his household, and around all that he has on every side? You have blessed the work of his hands, and his possessions have increased in the land. But now, stretch out Your hand and touch all that he has, and he will surely curse You to Your face!" And the Lord said to Satan,

"Behold, all that he has is in your power; only do not lay a hand on his person" (Job 1:8-12a).

First, he murdered his farm animals, then all 10 of his children, then he infected him with itchy/painful boils. All Job could do was sit in misery and scrape those putrid puss pockets off himself while his friends tried to get him to confess whatever sin(s) he must have committed to get in this horrendous condition and his wife told him to curse God. Satan was not allowed to kill him. But, regarding Jesus, he did not have that restriction. In fact, it was part of the plan and Jesus knew it.

As the god of this world, it was now his time. This time the lions would rip Him to pieces, unlike with Daniel. This time the fiery furnace would burn every cell in His body, unlike with the children of Judah—Hananiah, Mishael, and Azariah. This time the digestive acid in the great fish would melt Jesus to the core, unlike with Jonah. All Satan had to do was choose which excruciating punishment to administer. But, did he have that choice really? Prophetically, Jesus' death was spelled out in detail for hundreds of years. God wanted no mistaking that anybody other than Jesus Christ was the true Savior of the world. The following represents just some of the prophecies fulfilled by Jesus:

* * *

Prophecy

When your days are fulfilled and you rest with your fathers, I will set up your seed after you, who will come from your body, and I will establish his kingdom. He shall build a house for My name, and I will establish the throne of his kingdom forever (2 Samuel 7:12-13).

"Behold, the days are coming," says the Lord, "That I will raise to David a Branch of righteousness; A King shall reign and prosper, And execute judgment and righteousness in the earth" (Jeremiah 23:5, B.C. 742).

Fulfillment

And when He had removed him, (Saul) He raised up for them David as king, to whom also He gave testimony and said, 'I have found David the son of Jesse, a man after my own heart, who will do all My will.' From this man's seed, according to the promise, God raised up for Israel a Savior—Jesus (Acts 13:22-23).

Concerning His Son Jesus Christ our Lord, who was born of the seed of David according to the flesh, and declared to be the Son of God with power according to the Spirit of holiness, by the resurrection from the dead (Romans 1: 3-4, A.D. 60).

Prophecy

Therefore the Lord Himself will give you a sign: Behold, the virgin shall conceive and bear a Son, and shall call His name Immanuel (Isaiah 7:14, B.C. 742).

Fulfillment

Now the birth of Jesus Christ was as follows: After His mother Mary was betrothed to Joseph, before they came together, she was found to be with child of the Holy Spirit. And she will bring forth a Son, and you shall call His name Jesus, for he will save His people from their sins (Matthew 1:18, 21, B.C. 5).

Prophecy

The Spirit of the Lord is upon Me, Because the Lord has anointed Me to preach good tidings unto the meek [poor]; He hath sent me to bind up the brokenhearted, To proclaim liberty to the captives, And the opening of the prison to those who are bound; To proclaim the acceptable year of the Lord (Isaiah 61:1, B.C. 698).

Fulfillment

"The Spirit of the Lord is upon me, Because He has anointed Me To preach the gospel to the poor; He has sent me to heal the brokenhearted, To proclaim liberty to the captives And recovery of sight to the blind, To set at liberty those that are oppressed; To proclaim the acceptable year of the Lord" (Luke 4:18-19, A.D. 2).

Prophecy

Nevertheless the gloom will not be upon her who is distressed, As when at first He lightly esteemed The land of Zebulun and the land of Nephtali, And afterward more heavily oppressed her, By the way of the sea, beyond the Jordan, In Galilee of the Gentiles. The people who walked in darkness Have seen a great light; Those who dwelt in the land of the shadow of death, Upon them a light has shined (Isaiah 9:1-2, B.C. 740).

Fulfillment

Now when Jesus heard that John had been put onto prison, He departed to Galilee. And leaving Nazareth, He came and dwelt in Capernaum, which is by the sea, in the regions of Zebulun and Naphtali, that it might be fulfilled which was spoken by Isaiah the prophet, saying: "The land of Zebulun and the land of Naphtali, By the way of the sea, beyond the Jordan, Galilee of the Gentiles: The people who sat in darkness have seen a great light, And upon those who sat in the region and shadow of death Light has dawned (Matthew 4:12-16, A.D. 27).

Prophecy

A bruised reed He will not break, And smoking flax He will not quench; He will bring forth justice for truth (Isaiah 42:3, B.C. 712).

Fulfillment

A bruised reed shall He not break, and smoking flax he shall not quench, till He send forth judgment unto victory (Matthew 12:20, A.D. 31).

Prophecy

Those that hate Me without a cause Are more than the hairs of mine head (Psalm 69:4a).

Fulfillment

If I had not done among them the works which no one else did, they would have no sin; but now they have seen and also hated both Me and My Father. But this happened that the Word might be fulfilled which is written in their law. "They hated Me without cause" (John 15:24-25).

Prophecy

Yes, mine own familiar friend, in whom I trusted, which did eat of my bread, hath lifted up his heel against Me (Psalm 41:9).

Fulfillment

I speak not of you all: I know whom I have chosen: but that the scripture may be fulfilled, He that eateth bread with me hath lifted up his heel against me (John 13:18, A.D. 33).

Prophecy

Then I said to them, "If it is agreeable to you, give Me My wages; and if not, refrain." So they weighed out for My wages thirty pieces of silver. And the Lord said to Me, "Throw it to the potter" – that princely price they set on Me. So I took the thirty pieces of silver and threw them into the house of the Lord for the potter (Zechariah 11: 12-13, B.C. 487).

To pay this shepherd 30 pieces of silver was an insult—this was the price paid to an owner for a slave gored by an ox. This is also the amount Judas received for betraying Jesus. The priceless Messiah was sold for the price of a slave.[68]

Fulfillment

Then one of the twelve, called Judas Iscariot, went to the chief priest, and said, "What are you willing to give me if I deliver Him to you?" And they counted out to him thirty pieces of silver (Matthew 26: 14-15, A.D. 33).

Then Judas, His betrayer, seeing that He had been condemned, was remorseful and brought back the thirty pieces of silver to the chief priests and elders, saying, "I have sinned by betraying innocent blood." And they said, "What is that to us? You see to it!" Then he threw down the pieces of silver in the temple and departed, and went and hanged himself. But the chief priests took the silver pieces and said, "It is not lawful to put them into the treasury, because they are the price of blood,". And they consulted together and bought with them the potter's field, to bury strangers in. Therefore that field has been called the Field of Blood to this day. Then was fulfilled what was spoken by Jeremiah the prophet, saying, "And they took the thirty pieces of silver, the value of Him who was priced, whom they of the children

---

68. Footnote from Zech. 11:12, *New King James Version: Life Application Study Bible* (United States: Tyndale House Publishers, Incorporated, 1996), pg. 1646.

of Israel priced, and gave them for the potter's field, as the Lord directed me" (Matthew 27:3-10, A.D. 33).

Prophecy

"Yet I have set My King On my holy hill of Zion." "I will declare the decree: The Lord has said to Me, 'You are My Son, Today I have begotten You' (Psalm 2:6-7).

Fulfillment

Pilate therefore said to Him, "Are You a king then?" Jesus answered, "You say rightly that I am a king, for this cause I was born, and for this cause I have come into the world, that I should bear witness to the truth. Everyone who is of the truth hears My voice" (John 18:37, A.D.33).

Prophecy

I gave my back to those who struck Me, And My cheeks to those who plucked out the beard; I did not hide my face from shame and spitting (Isaiah 50:6, B.C. 712).

Fulfillment

Then some [High priests] began to spit on Him, and to blindfold Him, and to beat Him, and to say to Him, "Prophesy!" And the officers struck Him with the palms of their hands (Mark 14:65).

Prophecy

They pierced My hands and My feet (Psalm 22:16B).

And I will pour on the house of David and on the inhabitants of Jerusalem the Spirit of grace and supplication; then they will look on Me whom they pierced, Yes, they will mourn for Him as one mourns for his only son, and grieve for him as one grieves for a firstborn (Zechariah 12:10, B.C. 487).

Fulfillment

But one of the soldiers with a spear pierced His side, and forthwith came there out blood and water. And again another scripture saith, They shall look on Him whom they pierced (John 19:34, 37, A.D. 33).

Behold, He is coming with clouds, and every eye will see Him, even they who pierced Him. And all the tribes of the earth will mourn because of Him. Even so, Amen (Revelation 1:7).

Prophecy

Therefore I will divide Him a portion with the great, And He shall divide the spoil with the strong, Because He poured out His soul unto death, and He was wounded with the transgressors, and He bore the sin of many, And made intercession for the transgressors (Isaiah 53:12, B.C. 712).

Fulfillment

With Him they also crucified two robbers, one on His right and the other on His left. So the scripture was fulfilled which says, "And He was numbered with the transgressors" (Mark 15:27-28, A.D. 33).

"For I say to you that this which is written must still be accomplished in Me: 'And He was numbered with the transgressors.' for the things concerning Me have an end" (Luke 22:37, A.D. 33).

For He made Him who knew no sin to be sin for us, that we might become the righteousness of God in Him (2 Corinthians 5:21, A.D. 33).

Prophecy

All they that see Me laugh Me to scorn, they shoot out the lip, they shake the head, saying, He trusted on the Lord that he would deliver him, let him deliver him, seeing he delighted in him (Psalm 22:7-8).

Fulfillment

And those who passed by blasphemed Him, wagging their heads and saying, "You who destroy the temple and build it in three days, save Yourself! If you are the son of God, come down from the cross." Likewise, the chief priests also, mocking with the scribes and elders, said, "He saved others; Himself He cannot save. If He is the King of Israel, let Him now come down from the cross, and we will believe Him. He trusted in God; let Him deliver Him now if He will have Him; for He said, 'I am the Son of God.'" Even the robbers who were crucified with Him reviled Him with the same thing (Matthew 27:39-44, A.D. 33).

Prophecy

They divide My garments among them, And for My clothing they cast lots (Psalm 22:18).

Fulfillment

Then they crucified Him, and divided His garments, casting lots, that it might be fulfilled which was spoken by the prophet: "They divided My garments among them, and for My clothing they cast lots" (Matthew 27:35, A.D. 33)

Prophecy

They also gave Me gall for My food, And for my thirst they gave me vinegar to drink (Psalm 69:21).

Fulfillment

They gave Him sour wine mingled with gall to drink. But when He tasted it, He would not drink (Matthew 27:34, A.D. 33).

Prophecy

My God, My God, why have You forsaken Me? Why are You so far from helping Me, and from the words of My groaning? (Psalm 22:1)

Fulfillment

Now from the sixth hour to about the ninth hour there was darkness over all the land. And about the ninth hour Jesus cried out with a loud voice saying, "Eli Eli, lama sabachthani?" that is, "My God, My God, why have You forsaken Me?" (Matthew 27:46, A.D. 33)

Prophecy

And the Lord said to Moses and Aaron, "This is the ordinance of the Passover: No foreigner shall eat it; In one house it shall be eaten; you shall not carry any of the flesh outside the house, nor shall you break one of its bones (Exodus 12:43, 46, B.C. 1491).

He guards all his bones; Not one of them is broken (Psalm 34:20).

Fulfillment

But when they came to Jesus and saw that He was already dead, they did not break His legs. For those things were done that the Scripture should be fulfilled, "Not one of His bones shall be broken" (John 19:33, 36, A.D. 33).

Prophecy

The Lord said to my Lord, "Sit at My right hand, Till I make Your enemies Your footstool" (Psalm 110:1).

Fulfillment

God...has in these last days spoken to us by His Son, whom He has appointed heir of all things, through whom also He made the worlds, who being the brightness of His glory and the express image of His person, and upholding all things by the word of His power, when He had by Himself purged our sins, sat down at the right hand of the Majesty on high (Hebrews 1:1-3, A.D. 60).[69]

* * *

Jesus knew Satan's plan would involve unimaginable pain, humiliation, and mutilation. Jesus also knew if He crumbled, all of mankind would suffer eternal punishment because the Savior was too weak to see the plan of redemption all the way through. I don't mean just cry out for 12 legions of angels to rescue Him off the cross, I mean to not sin during this whole ordeal. Not one curse word, not one mean thought, no hate in His heart—only forgiveness, making Jesus the strongest Man who has ever lived. Behold the hour is at hand.

---

69. "A Study in Prophecy," Jewish Voice Broadcast, PO Box 6, Phoenix, AZ.

Chapter Eleven

Forgive Them, Father: The Sacrificial Lamb

I t was 15 Nissan, Erev Pesach, the eve of Passover, and Jesus was about to serve the "Last Supper." Every prophecy had been fulfilled except those pertaining to His crucifixion, burial, and resurrection. According to the Judeans, the Jewish day actually began at sunset the day before. Friday began on Thursday sundown (nightfall between 4:30 PM–6:00 PM) to Friday sundown. Even in the western world we begin each day at midnight, so the concept is not strange to us.[70]

Jesus, having just served the Last Supper (later to be called the first communion) on the day of preparation before the Passover Sabbath, led His inner circle, John, James, and Peter, to a secluded spot known by His disciples on the Mount of Olives in the Garden of Gethsemane.

It seemed like any other night, cold but not freezing. Jesus wasn't Himself. He was actually glistening from what appeared to be crimson colored sweat.

---

70. Zola Levitt, "Zola Explains the Three Days and Three Nights," Levitt.com, accessed March 12, 2021, https://porchofthelord.com.

And being in an agony He prayed more earnestly; and His sweat became as it were great drops of blood falling down upon the ground (Luke 22:44).

Meanwhile, His inner circle of friends couldn't keep their eyes open. How He longed for them to pray while the greatest betrayal known to Man was taking place. Yet at Jesus' greatest hour of need He thought not of Himself but encouraged them to sleep for the remaining minutes.

Then comes He to the disciples, and says to them, Sleep on now, and take your rest: behold, the hour is at hand, and the Son of man is betrayed into the hands of sinners (Matthew 26:45).

Confronted by an angry mob armed with swords and clubs, the quiet teacher immediately bore the cup from which less than an hour before He sought release, so His disciples could go their way. The cup means the suffering, isolation, and death that Jesus would have to endure in order to atone for the sins of the world.[71] The next hour was a whirlwind of events: Jesus was betrayed by one of His own, performed an ear transplant, told the mob twice that it was He they sought because they kept falling over themselves when He identified Himself as "I AM" (an affirmation of Deity[72]), then was denied and/or deserted by His closest friends. Jesus knew He would be betrayed by one of His disciples, disowned by another, and deserted by all of them for a time.[73] He knew He would be beaten, belittled, and tormented publicly. Still, "He loved them to the end" (John 13:1). The worst for Jesus was yet to come.

Behold, we go up to Jerusalem; and the son of man shall be betrayed unto the chief priests, and unto the scribes, and they

---

71. Footnote from John 18:11, *New King James Version: Life Application Study Bible* (United States: Tyndale House Publishers, Incorporated, 1996), 1945.

72. Warren Wiersbe, *Bible Exposition Commentary,* Vol. 1 (United States: Victor Books, 2003), 373.

73. Footnote from John 13:1, *New King James Version: Life Application Study Bible* (United States: Tyndale House Publishers, Incorporated, 1996), 1935.

shall condemn Him to death, And shall deliver Him to the Gentiles to mock, and to scourge, and to crucify Him: and the third day he shall rise again (Matthew 20:18-19).

And while He was still speaking, behold Judas, one of the twelve, with a great multitude with swords and clubs, came from the chief priests and elders of the people (Matthew 26:47).

Jesus therefore, knowing all things that would come upon Him, went forward and said to them, "Whom are you seeking?" They answered Him, "Jesus of Nazareth." Jesus said to them, "I am He." And Judas who betrayed Him, also stood with them. Now when He said to them, "I am He", they drew back and fell to the ground. Then He asked them again, "Whom are you seeking?" And they said Jesus of Nazareth." Jesus answered, "I have told you that I am He. Therefore, if you seek Me, let these go their way. Shall I not drink the cup which My Father has given me?" (John 18:4-8, 11b)

TRAVESTY # 1—Rabid Desires

Pushed and shoved to Caiaphas' house, appointed by Rome as the succeeding high priest to his father-in-law Annas, Jesus found Himself to be the leading Man in a contrived dog and pony show. Totally illegal, the Pharisaic council conducted an informal hearing in the dark of night to appease their rabid desire to place culpability on their number one nemesis. This hearing was full of illegalities that made a mockery of justice.[74] Jesus endured an "all-nighter" of accusations by false witnesses in their hopes of obtaining evidence pointing to the charge they sought—blasphemy. Uncannily, Jesus remained silent throughout most of the drama, the first of many silences until

---

74. Footnote from "The six stages of Jesus' Trial", *New King James Version: Life Application Study Bible* (United States: Tyndale House Publishers, Incorporated, 1996), 1947.

asked point blank whether he was the Son of God, the Messiah. He answered in the affirmative.

> And they that had laid hold on Jesus led Him away to Caiaphas the high priest, where the scribes and the elders were assembled. And the high priest arose, and said unto him, Answerest thou nothing? What is it which these witness against thee? But Jesus held his peace, And the high priest answered and said unto Him, I adjure thee by the living God, that thou tell us whether thou be the living Christ, the Son of God. Jesus saith unto him, Thou hast said... (Matthew 26:57, 62-64a).

Tearing his garment in dramatic display, Caiaphas banged his oral gavel, rendering Jesus guilty of sacrilege worthy of death. As their leader, Caiaphas allowed some of the more hostile guards to challenge the popular prophet during a "game" of guess who. Hurling inflammatory insults they covered His head and proceeded to spit, shove, spin, then punch their long-awaited Messiah, jeering, "Prophesy. Who hit you?" Having traveled to Israel, I was surprised to see the "Prophecy Game" from two thousand years before etched into the stone entrance floor along the "Way of the Cross."

> Then the high priest tore his clothes and said, "He has spoken blasphemy! Why do we need any more witnesses? Look, now you have heard the blasphemy. What do you think?" "He is worthy of death," they answered. Then they spit in His face and struck him with their fists. Others slapped him and said, "Prophesy to us, Christ. Who hit you?" (Matthew 26:65-68)

TRAVESTY # 2: Herod

This charade continued until morning, when Jesus was delivered bound to the Roman prefect, Pontius Pilate. Inside the Praetorian chambers where Pilate was unhappily assigned in the "stinking" Jerusalem district to keep peace and order for the past 11 years, he finally got to meet this so-called "King of the Jews." He conducted his own type of trial, an informal inquiry (Pilate's first mistake). Jesus remained silent again until asked, "Are you the King of the Jews?" This exchange waxed philosophical, leaving Pilate in a dilemma about Jesus' version of truth. Pilate's weakness in integrity and grit began to show when he engaged the angry Jews rather than the Roman court. He was well on his way to losing the battle between strength in leadership and cowardly, irreparable submission. In an act of desperation, Pilate sent Jesus to be examined by Herod, tetrarch of the province of Galilee and Perea, because much of Jesus' ministry was in the Galilee region.

Herod Antipas, son of "Herod the Great," had much going for him but even more going against him. He was a reputable architect over several cities including the capitol, Tiberius. He rebuilt the second temple, initially built by Ezra and Nehemiah, 500 years after the destruction of Solomon's first temple by the Babylonians. Despite any political or architectural accomplishments, Herod is best known for marrying his own brother Philip's wife, beheading John the Baptist, and severely persecuting the church. No matter what flattery Herod imposed upon Jesus, he was unsuccessful in engaging Him. Jesus neither looked at nor spoke to him during their brief encounter. God forbid you or I ever get in this position.

TRAVESTY #3: The Crowd

Foolishly, Pilate held his own brand of public election between an insurrectionist named Barabbas and an alleged king named Jesus (Pilate's second mistake). The well learned and much admired priests and elders chose the murderer over the life giver. As an appeasement offering, in order to avoid internal rebellion among the Jews and possibly face Roman Emperor Tiberius' dissatisfaction, he offered to torment Jesus whom he found to be innocent. A callous but shallow man, Pilate resorted to inflicting ungodly physical pain on God Himself as a token offering to satisfy the ferocious appetite of the insanely jealous religious leaders (Pilate's third mistake).

So then Pilate took Jesus and scourged Him. And the soldiers twisted a crown of thorns and put it on His head, and
they put on Him a purple robe. Then they said to Him, "Hail,
King of the Jews!" and they struck Him with their hands
(John 19:1-3).

TRAVESTY #4: The Scourge

The scourging is a horrific narrative promulgated by Pilate. It is very
graphic and only for the reader who can withstand the violence perpetrated
on the body of the Son of Man. I utilize the disclaimer that the following
could have happened this way. There are many versions, but in every case
I do not know how Jesus survived it except in order to fulfill the scriptures,
crucifixion had to follow.

Christ hath redeemed us from the curse of the law, being
made a curse for us: for it is written, Cursed is everyone that
hangeth on a tree (Galatians 3:13).

Tied to a two-foot-high granite whipping post with hands secured to a
metal ring where movement was extremely limited, it cannot be reported
with certainty that Jesus only received 40 lashes save one. According to Jewish law this would be mandatory in order to get the count right, provided the
victim survived that long. Many did not. Rome was not bound to Jewish law.
Until the *exactor mortis*, the supervisor of death, raised his hand to stop, the
floggers continued striking and ripping away at flesh unmercifully.

Two torturers stood behind Him, one on the left, the other on the right.
Simultaneously they thrust the flagrum or Roman whip toward the shoulders, working their way down the back and legs. Sometimes they would
stop the thongs before reaching their merciful end only to savagely yank the
hooks from wherever they were deeply inserted, taking with it huge pieces
of human flesh, exposing organs, muscles, sinews, bowels, or wherever they
were hooked. These flagrums or flagellums were no ordinary instruments
of torture. They consisted of a leather grip with three to nine leather thongs

216

possibly as long as three feet. Each thong had lead spikes, sharp bone and glass shards, and bronze or marble coils—hooks designed to pull back the skin. If the skin was not ripped off it hung there like long ribbons. They were known as scorpion whips, the most feared weapon of that time. "This instrument was designed to lacerate and humiliate. The weighed thongs struck the skin so violently that it broke open."[75] Each slash cut so deeply it literally raked the Man's insides as if plowing a field.

> The plowers plowed upon my back: they made long their furrows (Psalms 129:3).

The method of shallow plowing versus deep involves breaking the sod, or in this case skin, two to four inches deep. Imagine long, two-inch furrows running up and down your body. There remains the possibility at one point during the excruciating scourge that when Jesus' lower body collapsed, He was flipped over and flayed from the neck down to His feet.

As this was a sloppy, callous blood bath, one can only imagine how much overlap of slashes there must have been, exposing organs and bone. This macabre display of line graphs all over His back resulted in one gaping wound leading to something beautiful for you and me—healing.

> But He was wounded for our transgressions, He was bruised for our iniquities: the chastisement of our peace was upon Him; and with His stripes we are healed. All we like sheep have gone astray; we have turned every-one to his own way; and the Lord hath laid on Him the iniquity of us all (Isaiah 53:5-6).

The Hebrew word for stripes is *chaburah*. It means "bruise, stripe, or wound." It could just as easily have read "by His wound we are healed." Have you ever wondered which wound this verse was referencing?

---

75. "The Scourging of Jesus," David McClister, Truth Magazine, published September 25, 2012, https://www.truthmagazine.com/?s=the+scourging+of+jesus.

It is no wonder that Jesus was unrecognizable as both a man and human being. The severity of the beating usually determined how long the victim would live on the cross. During the final trial, the torturer had taken Jesus to the very brink of death. His body and face had been so thrashed and mangled He was unrecognizable.[76] Jesus knew his whole life that He would be beaten to the point where He no longer looked like a human being. The Christ would willingly subject Himself to all kinds of humiliation and scorn.[77] The worst for Jesus was still to come.

> I gave my back to those who struck Me, and My cheeks to those who plucked out the beard; I did not hide My face from shame and spitting (Isaiah 50:6).

> As many were astonied at thee; his visage was so marred more than any man, and his form more than the sons of men (Isaiah 52:14).

TRAVESTY #5: Pontius Pilate

The Crowning: Having finished with Jesus in the outside whipping court "of blood," Pilate's pernicious soldiers (a massive number comprising a garrison) took Him into the common hall to have a little fun. They took flexible vines with sharp, two-inch thorns and embedded a hastily woven crown onto his head. The blood poured down His face onto His neck and shoulders. At this point He was unrecognizable. Pilate left them to their devices; they became like thirsty vultures feeding on their hatred for the Jews. The satire of this whole hellish affair was affixing a scarlet robe over His wounded shoulders and open back and placing a reed in his right hand while taunting Him with, "Hail, King of the Jews!" Then they spit on Him one by one, pulled out His beard, and took the reed and pummeled him on the head with it, driving the thorns in further, fully mocking the Savior of the world (Matt. 27: 27-31).

76. "Gather, Grow, Goo. Just Jesus Series; It's Not Too Late!" Union Baptist of IVA, accessed March 28, 2021.

77. "How Christ's Final Day Changes your Everyday," Mike McKinley, TheGoodBook.com, published March 31, 2015.

Pilate put Him on display once more hoping to appease the bloodthirsty crowd. This only served to incite them further. Full blown jealousy gave way to rage to the point where they accepted His blood on their heads and the heads of their children. The Jews took full advantage when they saw Pilate weakening and played their final card—Caesar. Rather than risk rebuke or worse from Caesar, Pilate acquiesced and released Jesus to impalement on a cross. Pilate's self-interest was stronger than his sense of justice,[78] Pilate's fourth mistake.

> Pilate saith unto them, What shall I do then with Jesus which is called Christ? They all said unto him, Let Him be crucified. And the governor said, Why, what evil hath He done? But they cried out the more, saying, Let Him be crucified. When Pilate saw that He could prevail nothing, but that rather a tumult was made, he took water, and washed his hands before the multitude, saying, I am innocent of the blood of this just person: see ye to it. Then answered all the people, and said, His blood be on us, and on our children (Matthew 27:22-25).

> Then Jesus came out, wearing the crown of thorns and the purple robe. And Pilate said to them, "Behold the Man!" Therefore, when the chief priests and officers saw Him, they cried out, saying, "Crucify Him, crucify Him!" …Now it was the Preparation Day of the Passover [Good Friday] and about the sixth hour. And he said to the Jews, "Behold your King!" But they cried out, "Away with Him, away with Him! Crucify Him!" Pilate said to them, "Shall I crucify your King?" The chief priests answered, We have no king but Caesar!" Then he delivered Him to be crucified. Then they took Jesus and led Him away (John 19:5-6,14-16).

78. Footnote from "The Six Stages of Jesus' Trial", *New King James Version: Life Application Study Bible* (United States: Tyndale House Publishers, Incorporated, 1996), 1947.

Pontius Pilate: The Roman prefect from A.D. 26-36, similar to the office of governor, hated his assignment and hated the Jews for whom he was responsible to keep the peace. They were an annoyance to him and he did only what was necessary to get by. The Jewish people understood what Pilate was—a cruel but ambitious opportunist who feared the authorities in Rome. It took very little to push his buttons. All they had to do was mention Caesar's title or name and they got what they wanted, except one time. The description hanging over Jesus' head on the cross announced His crime. He was not the typical deserter, rebel, or runaway slave deserving of capital punishment according to Roman standards. He was guilty of being the King of the Jews. Pilate could not override God's will.

> Now Pilate wrote a title and put it on the cross. And the writing was: JESUS OF NAZARETH, THE KING OF THE JEWS. Then many of the Jews read this title, for the place where Jesus was crucified was near the city; and it was written in Hebrew, Greek, and Latin. Therefore, the chief priests of the Jews said to Pilate, "Do not write, 'The King of the Jews' but, 'He said, "I am the King of the Jews."' Pilate answered, "What I have written I have written" (John 19:19-22).

Except for taking a strong stance on the sign and allowing the priests to post guards in front of a dead Man's tomb, we hear no more of Pilate. What shall we say of Pilate's legacy? Is it one of innocence since he washed his hands of any guilt before the bloodthirsty crowd demanding Jesus' crucifixion? Or does his legacy reflect the bloodiest of any authoritarian under Roman rule? He remains the self-proclaimed guiltless ruler responsible for all the bloodshed unto death of the sacrificial Lamb of God.

220

Why Was Good Friday Good?

While the cross represents the worst part of Jesus' crucifixion, including the interrogations, fake trial, punching, scourging, spitting, mocking, etc., it also represents the best part. As a little girl attending the Roman Catholic church, I distinctly remember slowly edging my way down the long pew. It was my intention to stand up and ask the priest why everyone called Good Friday good. What was good about God dying on a splintery old cross? Why didn't they call it bad Friday? The name Good Friday is entirely appropriate because the suffering and death of Jesus, as terrible as it was, marked the dramatic culmination of God's plan to save His people from their sins. "We...have to understand the bad news of our condition as sinful people under condemnation." We are enslaved [to sin]. The wrath of God against sin had to be poured out on Jesus, the perfect sacrificial substitute [because He Himself had never sinned] in order for forgiveness and salvation to be poured out to the nations. Paradoxically, the day that seemed to be the greatest triumph of evil was actually the death blow in God's glorious good plan to redeem the world from bondage. We receive divine forgiveness, mercy, and peace because Jesus willingly took our divine punishment, the result of God's righteousness against sin. Good Friday marks the day when wrath and mercy met at the cross.[79]

Looking unto Jesus, the author and finisher of our faith, who for the joy that was set before Him endured the cross, despising the shame, and has sat down at the right hand of the throne of God (Hebrews 12:2).

---

79. "What's so Good about Good Friday?", Justin Holcomb, Christianity.com, published February 17, 2022, https://www.christianity.com/god/jesus-christ/what-s-so-good-about-good-friday.html.

TRAVESTY #6: The Crucifixion

After the parody of worship performed by the Roman soldiers, Jesus was led to the cross, which He was expected to carry for approximately one half mile. This path, known as the "Way of the Cross," was uphill and rocky. It was customary for the criminal to carry his cross, or at least the crossbeam, from the hall of judgment to the place of execution, "The Skull."[80] The place of the skull, *Golgotha* in Hebrew, is so properly named. Today, atop a ghoulish rock, two huge holes appear as empty sockets that stare down at a thriving bus station just outside the city, where people come and go all day long. I was there twice and each time I found it to be formidable and grim.

The cross was so heavy that it was theorized to be divided into two pieces—the *patibulum* or crossbeam and *stipe* or vertical upright beam. The beam alone could have weighed 45 to 300 pounds. Either way, Jesus was entirely too weak from his beatings and loss of blood to carry or even drag this monstrosity very far. The upright beams would typically already be in position at the site of execution. So, it is most likely the case that Jesus only carried the horizontal beam. During the process of crucifixion, nails were driven into the carpus, the bones of the wrist. This exercise of torture crushed the bones and nerves, serving minimal support for the heavily hanging body. The victim and crossbeam were then lifted up about 9 to 12 feet into the air and mounted on the top of the vertical beam.[81]

One thing is certain—this tree was destined to be the most famous tree in all of history. The tree that bore the Man and the sins of the world for all generations. There has never been a tree or cross more talked, written, filmed, or sung about than this one, including imitation artifacts/jewelry made. "Jesus was to bear the curse of the law and become a curse for us; and in order to do this, He had to hang on a tree."[82]

---

80. Warren Wiersbe, *Bible Exposition Commentary*, Vol. 1 (United States: Victor Books, 2003), 382.
81. "Crucifixion," *Encyclopedia Britannica*, published October 12, 2018, https://www.britannica.com/topic/crucifixion-capital-punishment.
82. Warren Wiersbe, *Bible Exposition Commentary*, Vol. 1 (United States: Victor Books, 2003), 377.

> Christ has redeemed us from the curse of the law, having
> become a curse for us (for it is written, "Cursed is every-
> one who hangs on a tree") (Galatians 3:13).

The stipe was either in one piece or two by the time He reached Golgotha. He Himself was dangerously weak, unrecognizable, and publicly
humiliated. Jesus was laid over what was a splintery, bloody, feces- and
urine-infested cross. His arms were stretched across the width of the
beam. Spikes of five or more inches were hammered directly into his
wrists and maybe even through the stipe in order to keep him from slip-
ping when the crossbeam was either hoisted onto a groove or the cross
was raised and dropped into its final resting place, a hole four feet deep.
Either scenario would jolt the upper body so badly as to rip both arms
out of their joints.

> I am poured out like water, and all my bones are out of
> joint: my heart is like wax; it is melted in the midst of my
> bowels (Psalms 22:14).

Then came the securing of the legs and feet. Of course, they had
to be bored into the stipe so the victim could breathe. Commonly one
foot was placed over the other with knees bent to the side and a five- to
nine-inch spike hammered between the second and third metatarsals,
crushing more nerves and firmly securing Him to the wood, thus allowing the victim to raise Himself in order to breathe. This alone was sheer
agony. Bleeding externally as well as internally made each hard-earned
breath that much closer to being the last. Inhalation applied pressure to
the respiratory, shoulder, and arm muscles, while exhalation and gravity
pulled downward causing the full weight of the body to rest on the feet.
This could result in shoulder dislocation, cramps, and sheer exhaustion.
Let us not forget Jesus' raw back was literally one huge open wound as
He rubbed up and down against the harsh and filthy grain of the wood
just to breathe.

When He looked down, He saw some loved ones crying and shocked from horror. He had become hideous not because of the wounds or even the blood that flowed from every crevice, but He had become sin and manifested every evil thought and deed committed by His very own creation. He saw soldiers gambling over his clothes; fellow Jews and onlookers feasting their eyes on his raw, broken body; and the religious leaders, the alleged role models of the people, shaking their heads, jeering, and taunting Him to come down if He could. Imagine how cold your heart must be to belittle a man impaled to a cross struggling just to breathe?

When a crucified sufferer could no long tolerate the pain of pushing up on his broken feet to breathe, the process of asphyxiation would lead to hyperventilation. The heart would pump harder and harder, desperately trying to provide blood to the affected areas, leading to cardiac arrest. Over a short period of time, the victim's heart would begin to fail. Next, the lungs would collapse; excess fluid would begin filling the lining of the heart and lungs. The ultimate death of crucifixion was the eventual drowning in one's own fluids.[83] Whether Jesus died due to asphyxiation, cardiac arrest, loss of blood, dehydration, shock, a combination of the above, or other is not relevant. The relatively short time He hung on the cross, less than six hours, confirms Jesus' control over His entire execution. It wasn't until He said, "It is finished," that it was over.

Jesus' death was by divine appointment. He willingly gave His life for us. His death was an atonement. He accomplished the work of redemption on the cross.[84]

> I am the good shepherd. The good shepherd gives his life
> for the sheep (John 10:11).

---

83. Rick Renner, "Crucified," video, 10:40, Rick Renner Ministries, accessed July 12, 2022, https://renner.org/videos/crucified/.

84. Warren Wiersbe, *Bible Exposition Commentary*, Vol. 1 (United States: Victor Books, 2003), 384.

Ten Thousand Angels[85]
Ray Overholt

They bound the hands of Jesus in the garden where He prayed; They led Him through the streets in shame. They spat upon the Saviour so pure and free from sin; they said, "Crucify Him; He's to blame." Upon His precious head they placed a crown of thorns; They laughed and said, "Behold the King". They struck Him and they cursed Him and mocked His holy name. All alone He suffered everything. When they nailed Him to the cross, His mother stood nearby; He said, "Woman, behold thy son!" He cried, "I thirst for water," but they gave Him none to drink. Then the sinful work of man was done. To the howling mob He yielded; He did not for mercy cry. The cross of shame He took alone. And when He cried, "It is finished," He gave Himself to die; Salvation's wondrous plan was done.

He could have called ten thousand angels, To destroy the world and set Him free.

He could have called ten thousand angels, But He died alone, for you and me.

Before His Spirit left His body, He had a few more things to do. They are as follows: number one, He wanted us to know how important it was to have God in our lives. I believe this was His greatest sorrow. He may not have calculated the cost of losing the presence of His

---

85. Ray Overholt is said to have been led to Christ by his own composition. He died on 9/14/2008 at the age of 84.

Father. He knew God through all of eternity; then, for six earthly hours, He was completely alone. Sin and God are not compatible, but Jesus chose our sins over oneness with His Father during His darkest hour. What on earth kept him going? You and me. Number two, He spoke through His pain and sorrow on our behalf and made one final request to God the Father to forgive us. Because we are all sinners, we all played a part in putting Jesus to death.[86] He knew by faith, no matter what, God was there. He knew God was, is, and always will be—faithful.

> If I ascend into heaven, You are there; If I make my bed
> in hell, behold, You are there (Psalm 139:8).

Number three, He secured the salvation personally of one more soul—the thief beside Him. Number four, He cared for His incredible mother who remained faithful to Him all her life. What detail, what strength, what love. His last words affirmed His trust in Almighty God and His own worthiness to be called God.

> Let this mind be in you which was also in Christ Jesus,
> who, being in the form of God, did not consider it rob-
> bery to be equal with God, but made Himself of no rep-
> utation, taking the form of a bondservant, and coming
> in the likeness of men. And being found in appearance
> as a man. He humbled Himself and became obedient to
> the point of death, even the death of the cross. There-
> fore, God also has highly exalted Him and given Him
> the name which is above every name, that at the name
> of Jesus every knee should bow, of those in heaven, and
> of those on earth, and of those under the earth, and that
> every tongue should confess that Jesus Christ is Lord, to
> the glory of God the Father (Philippians 2:5-11).

---

86. Footnote from Luke 22:34, *New King James Version: Life Application Study Bible* (United States: Tyndale House Publishers, Incorporated, 1996), 1888.

It has been asked, "Why did He have to endure so much? Wasn't it enough He be crucified for our sins? Why the scorn, the brutal beating, the scourging, the crown, the humiliation, the unspeakable suffering?"

This kind of selflessness portrays the greatest of all men and the unconditional love of a Savior. The extent to which Jesus willingly suffered testifies to the depth of His love. You were redeemed "with the precious blood of Christ, as of a lamb without blemish and without spot" (1 Peter 1:19). His actions, deeds, and sufferings were all summarized in His final request: "Father, forgive them." As our sacrificial Lamb, He was saying, "I have shown *you* My love. I did all of this for you, every one of you, because I love you." The best for Jesus was yet to come—you and me.

> Greater love has no one than this, than to lay down one's life for his friends. "You are my friends..." (John 15:13-14a).

Epilogue

The multifaceted diamond of God's redemptive love has been laid out for you. Now it's up to you to study it from every angle. Throughout this book, certain individuals were chosen to exemplify Elohim in a human manner beholden to a firm but merciful, loving Father and God. Slow down a little to absorb and assimilate all that was presented to you. It is enough for you to choose which way you will go. Remember, He made you. He wanted you to be a part of His carefully planned eternity. He knew you from beginning to end before you were formed in your mother's womb. He loves you. He's waiting for you. What are you waiting for?

Choose you this day whom ye will serve…but as for me and my house, we will serve the Lord (Joshua 24:15).

About the Author

Growing up an only child, Cheryl Palermo lived a relatively secluded life with her parents. She attended Trenton State College and graduated with a BA, M.Ed, and multiple certificates in teaching, supervision, and administration with an emphasis in special education and music.

Cheryl gave her life to the Lord at thirty-one years old, and since that time she endeavored to become more like Jesus. Today, Cheryl is widowed and lives with her two children and two grandchildren. Her life is full and her number one passion is to encourage everyone to turn to Christ.

Cheryl can be contacted at cheryljpalermo@gmail.com.

Printed in the USA
CPSIA information can be obtained
at www.ICGtesting.com
JSHW012110120923
48301JS00006B/17